# The Surprising Power of Joy

## *Jouissance, Joie de Vivre*

Dr. James E. McReynolds

Joyologist and Minister of Joy to the World

Parson's Porch Books

*The Surprising Power of Joy: Jouissance, Joie de Vivre*
ISBN: Softcover 978-1-960326-71-3
Copyright © 2024 by James McReynolds

**Parson's Porch Books** is an imprint of Parson's Porch *&* Company (PP*&*C) in Cleveland, Tennessee. PP*&*C is a self-funded charity which earns money by publishing books of noted authors, representing all genres. Its face and voice is **David Russell Tullock** (dtullock@parsonsporch.com).

Parson's Porch *&* Company *turns books into bread & milk* by sharing its profits with the poor.

www.parsonsporch.com

# The Surprising Power of Joy

# DEDICATION

To those who share joy

with Jesus Christ and his followers who have encountered

Jesus through the Word of God.

# Contents

Foreword.................................................................9
Introduction..........................................................11
  Joy Delights!
Chapter One .........................................................15
  Joy Empowers!
Chapter Two..........................................................31
  Joy Relates!
Chapter Three........................................................38
  Joy Feels!
Chapter Four..........................................................46
  Joy Fulfills!
Chapter Five...........................................................59
  Joy Listens!
Chapter Six............................................................65
  Joy Hopes!
Chapter Seven .......................................................76
  Joy Serves!
Chapter Eight ........................................................83
  Joy Reads!
Chapter Nine .........................................................89
  Joy Celebrates!
Chapter Ten...........................................................95
  Joy Plays!
Chapter Eleven .....................................................108
  Joy Sings!
Chapter Twelve .....................................................122
  Joy Shares!
Chapter Thirteen....................................................131
  Joy Enjoys!
Chapter Fourteen ..................................................138
  Joy Lasts!
Bibliography .........................................................151
About the Author...................................................160

# Foreword

I have never known anyone so obsessed with the subject of joy as my old friend James McReynolds. When I read his books about joy, I have the feeling that his whole being is somehow absorbed in his one great human emotion.

His writings simply exude the perpetual excitement he experiences at merely contemplating the subject. His scholarly approach will contribute to infamy as years from now his work will holds its value.

I envy that. Jim must live continuously on the verge of tingling and shouting at the mention of the word. He is indeed a "joyologist," as he has styled himself.

He is someone whole life has been devoted to and absorbed in his one vitally important human emotion. Apparently, Jim and his wife Laurel live in a constant state of enjoyment. They become instantly excited at the thought of it.

Their home must glow with a special aura. I can't imagine what it would be like living next to one of the world's great generators, so that the atmosphere would hum with the power and energy emitted by their love and excitement.

Jim's readers can feel this. They can sense it after reading even a page or two of his latest book. The emotion is almost beyond infectious. Sharing his joy permeates the entire atmosphere of the words as they arise from the paper on which they are printed.

Let's face it. Most of us live in rather joyless worlds. We deal with countless problems of all kinds including overwork, a lack of work, shortage of funds, and many varieties of illnesses. Some things soluble and some not.

There are times when we feel simply overwhelmed and don't know where to turn or what to do. Joy is the last thing we think about. It seems like the wisp of a dream, something beyond our comprehension, much less something applicable to our very desperate existence.

This is true for Jim as it is for the rest of us. He and Laurel undoubtedly have their problems, sometimes in abundance. Nobody can escape them all of the time.

However, they have found the magic key that can instantly transform their situations from dire to beautiful. The moment when they stop thinking about the negative things that come into their lives and concentrate instead on the potentially positive things, the whole landscape changes dramatically.

Suddenly life is overflowing with love and beauty and possibility.

Most of us will never achieve this rare and glorious ability to alter our situations. But reading Jim's books will help us to do that. Just seeing how he thinks and being willing to envision the shining possibilities in our own lives is a big step in the right direction.

I know that when I read one of his books, or even a part of one, I feel a frisson of excitement about the things that are open to me. They were there all along, of course, but suddenly they become apparent to me and I see everything in an exciting new light.

I don't know any other author who possesses his kind of revelatory power. So I am more than happy to recommend this book, and all of Jim's books as well as something that can change your life. It really can. Just give it a chance.

--**Dr. John R. Killinger** is a retired professor, pastor, and writer of worldwide renown. He lives with his wife Gloria in Warrenton, Virginia.

# Introduction

# Joy Delights!

Joy is to delight in the divine. Psalm 34:8. Life brings some joyless moments. I have been obsessed by joy. Philippians 3:1. My own obsession does not deny tragedies or make light of any atrocity. The psalmist says that God keeps a record of our sorrows. Psalm 56:7-9.

I have always wanted to write. When I attended the University of Missouri School of Journalism, the possibility of ministering through writing became exciting and incredible.

My calling as Minister of Joy of the World is not to impress but to delight. Power in Writing

I became delighted in writing because God needed me to serve by writing. I am a writer because needs me to do it. Many of my books are a combination of spirituality and psychology. Work and spirit are closely connected.

Writing takes so much discipline, energy, and devotion. I enjoy the process of making this particular book the best I can make it. I don't have to be perfect when I am writing. I let go of the end results and focus on the work itself. The printed word still challenges lives.

Joy does not ignore reality. Joy does not depend on our circumstances. Joy is not a fleeting emotion. Joy is not meant to be elusive. God is good to us all the time. Psalm 118:1. The joy we have is glorious and inexpressible. I have become a prolific writer. Some think my obsession with writing is weird.

My old friends in ministry said that I do ministry like "two sheets in the wind." Preaching is another one of my obsessions. Some called me a preaching machine. God gives me the energy to do much more than is required or expected.

God is always by our side and on our side. Joy and faith are glued together. The joy Christ gives us is like sunshine on our darkest days. The warmth overwhelms us. As we bask in the beams of joy, all things become possible. Through the power of the Spirit, we receive strength. Isaiah 61:10.

We are works in progress. God treasures our trust. Psalm 62:5-8. God meets us where we are, just as we are. Realize the empowerment of joy. Rejoicing is easier when we are receiving good news.

Life is magnificent. Writers can say, "Wow," often. We fall out of our love for writing when we lose our wonder. Life fascinates us. Love is a wow. It is a wonder.

Life is a delight. God delights in us. God replaces duty with delight. If we are to release joy, we must release love. We become love. To become love, we must receive love. To delight is to experience being loved. I John 4:19.

The magic of writing, the joy of it, comes from balance. Writing is my oldest and dearest friend. Me and my computer and the page I am now composing, connect in a close relationship. We delight through our relationship with God and those close to our heart. We delight in our children and friends, and we find joy in being married.

Your spouse meets your needs. An effective, joy-filled marriage is motivated by internal factors. Commitment to another means to sacrifice, to serve with love. Both are always truthful and both do everything for the sake of intimacy to bring more genuine joy tat can be imagined. Delight takes love to a higher level.

Married life becomes a pleasure and a privilege. When the commitment runs deep, it is a delight to love, serve, and give to one another. Love is the baseline. It becomes not our duty, but it is our desire. Couple who no longer say, "I have to." They declare, I want to."

That is the desired development from duty to delight. These couples share a common relationship of eternal joy. Most people who engage in marriage find that often it is reality to love something or another human being without being delightfully passionate about them. After ten or twenty years of marriage, they find their love and joy has not been grown with satisfaction through the years.

In a scene in my favorite Civil War movie, Shenandoah, Jimmy Stewart is talking with a young man who asks him about marrying his daughter. Stewart says, "Do you like her?" He replies, "Well, sir, I love her?"

"No, I didn't say if you love her, I said, do you like her." Stewart goes on to share that he liked his departed wife Martha, but only in the last years, he shared that he had come to love her.

Faith takes us beyond our comfort zone. Focus on the reality of God. We can re-learn or learn how to delight in the perfection of God. Whatever happens is subject to the will of God. Joy happens in times of sorrow. We delight in the presence and purpose of the Divine. The power to continue rejoicing comes with continuing fellowship with the One who gives joy. Commit to staying connected to the Word of God, the Holy Spirit, and Jesus. After 35 years of marital delight, we have been enabled to be constantly transformed into happy lovers who work longer, harder, and with a belief in eternal delight.

Miriam Winter, a Catholic nun, wrote a song that reflects the gift of joy. "I saw raindrops on my window. Joy is like the rain. Laughter runs across my pain, Slips away and comes again. Joy is like the rain." (Nancy Mace and Peter Rabins, *The 36-Hour Day*, p. 213) Joy delights!

# Chapter One
# Joy Empowers!

Joy empowers us. Joy raises our frequency. Joy permits us to attract more that we truly desire. Yet how often will deny ourselves joy. Experiencing joy for ourselves is never taking it from others. Our culture is focused on lack and scarcity. Feeling joyful causes some to feel guilty. Beyond feeling worthy. External living causes depression and anger. We make poor decisions.

Internal living because of our struggles "to do the right thing." We do not believe that we are worthy of being joyful. If we have joy, we come to feel guilty. We think we are betraying family and friends if they are experiencing a hard time. (Melissa Joy Jonsson, *The Art of Limitless Living*, pp. 1-23)

Joy is never selfish. How we feel differing human feelings. At the core, we humans are made of energy. Energy vibrates at different frequencies. High energy is empowering. Low energy disempowers.

Consciousness creates reality. Like attracts like. We draw more joyful things and joyful people. We laugh when somebody laughs. We have no clue, but we smile.

Regardless of your age, jump up and down to increase your blood flow and bring the energy of God. Imagine a reflection of a moment of joy. What would a stranger notice about you if they encountered you on a day when you experienced joy?

## "Joy in Life"

*Joie de Vivre* in French means "joy in life." In practical words, it means making moments special, bringing more joy into our lives and into the lives of others. Of all the places, my wife

Laurel and I have traveled to, France is a favorite. Laurel enjoyed attending a cooking school in a chateau. I shared joy empowerment messages at the military and naval academies in France. Some cultures experience more joy than others. What might happen in your life journey if you could be this joyful person more often?

## Joy: A Mystery to Be Lived

Life is a mystery to be lived. Most humans go on working long and boring hours. We just accept our feeling bad. The French long ago declared that that is not normal. Disempowering others with greed and corruption is common for those in power. Children of God, claim your joy. Joy empowers us to create wonders. When we feel empowered, we spread the feeling to others. That builds more positive feelings. Positive feelings dissolve negative feelings. Feeling empowered gives us incredible lives. Be present in the now.

Research results from various universities rarely focus on the spiritual aspects of *jouissance*. As for the senses *jouissance* means something like food, drink, sex, and touch in much of the research.
The power of jouissance as joy is discovered in a few places. Saint Francis defined eternal joy as a way we are destined to live. Joy and conversion is a phrase used to show an intense change. This time is a period of individual belief and divine identity. Pleasure and displeasure converge in Saint Francis' teaching and preaching. Saint Francis included illustrations about birds, ice, fire, the human body, spirit, and soul, lepers, and all creation to speak of change in a predictable direction.

His preaching animated a sense of perfect jouissance which suggested that conversion entails realignments between pleasure and unpleasure. Francis understood the jouissance of conversion as the experience he called "perfect joy."
There are certain places where joy sits closer to the surface.

16

Certain cultures such as in France support finding joy and expressing it. Guilty pleasures are a rare thing for most of us. The French rarely deny the body's invitation to pleasure. Pleasure and *joie de vivre* are related. After a delicious meal, the French ask, "Did the meal please you?" (Taras Lesiv, "Francis of Assisi's Perfect Jouissance," *Material Religion: The Journal of Objects, Art, and Belief*)

My daughter Linda and her husband Bill are vacationing in Paris as I am in my home office writing his book. There is now some rioting in Paris and much of France. She is fluent in French helped by her degree in French both at the University of Missouri and with classes at the University of Lyon.

Joy is the North Star for the French. They incite the joy of living. Nature and gardens are important to the French people. They see beauty as power. The French do not ask for permission to do things. Their thoughts are related to the fact we have so little time on this earth. Time is to be spent feeling joy. Enjoy nature. Be center as you breathe in creation. Each season has a smell. Watch the birds. Drink a warm cup of coffee on a cold winter day. Smile.
Smiles turn frowns upside down. Smiles change our bodies and spirits. Smiles ooze with a message to the brain that you are content. Joy is a concept capable of stopping people in their tracts. Talking about joy invites us to reflect on the meaning and life-giving aspects of our existence.

Joy draws humans to each other. Chris Meadows argues that joy is the first emotion to emerge in healthy human development. Meadows give his definition of joy as "the emotion which comes when one has grasped a good, or fulfilled a strong desire that is crucial to a person's own flourishing, the by-product of fulfilling her or his deepest longings." (Chris M. Meadows, *A Psychological Perspective on Joy and Emotional Fulfillment*, pp. 99-139)

Chris Meadows did research at Princeton University under the direction of Seward Hilton, the famous theologian. Any psychology of joy requires a theology of joy.

Joy is the most empowering emotions in the spectrum of what we feel as human beings. Joy can seem elusive. We are born with the capacity for joy. Joy events are wonderful as joy is a positive feeling. Our brains are wired to find positive feelings. We were made to seek joy. We reach out for a soft blanket that comforts our skin. We seek out a person who treats us in a loving way.

If joy is loaded often, it becomes easier and easier to load it again. Joy is like language fluency. A child born into a bi-lingual family will by default become bi-lingual. It is not a conscious choice on the part of the brain. It just happens. If the child uses a second language less and less, it will become hard to speak or understand the language.

The concept of fluency helps us understand that lack of joy in childhood. Their lives may not have deep patterns of joy. Any human being can immerse themselves in the language of joy and become fluent in all it entails.

The shift from trying to get through the day to trying to enjoy each day is hugely empowering. Our impulse is to restrain joy. As much as seek joy, we get freaked out once we feel joy. The present moments present possibilities for fresh joy. The power of those joy-filled times come as a pleasant surprise. The power of joy emerges in our lives in little flashes and glimpses. Joy washes over us like a sudden wave. Joy peals like a child's laughter. Joy pops in, then joy is out of view, like a finch flitting through the branches of an oak. Joy appears gently, like the turning up of one corner of our mouth. Joy flutters like an aspen leaf in a cool breeze. Joy flickers like sunlight peering through an open crack.

Joy flirts like a teen-age lover. Joy swishes like a three-point shot. Joy wavers in and out of our range. Joy flashes and fades like lightning on a hilltop. Joy brightens like a child's ice cream cone. Joy glows like a summer sunset. Joy astonishes like a vivid dream. Joy splashes like a cool fountain. Joy captures the joy of play.

We cannot wait for circumstances to bring us joy. Inner contentment and awareness of our purpose. Joy has more to do wit remaining in the presence of Jesus than with avoiding our problems. Philippians 4:11-13. Joy has nothing to do with eliminating negative circumstances. We embrace these struggles as opportunities to strengthen our faith. Only Jesus can empower our lives to flourish.

Joy becomes a filter to make it possible for people to flourish in well- being. We see with new eyes. We hear with new ears. Joy changes our perspective and perception of all circumstances. We will gain an eternal mind-set.

We recognize God in those divine moments. God is available to us. God's joy lifts our spirits and helps us with power and grace. Joy is an ongoing reminder that God is in control.

As joy grows in our hearts, it infiltrates our souls as our joys impact others, so we fully love God and our neighbor. Joy lifts others up. Despair brings people down. This empowering joy of Jesus makes us more approachable and relatable. Our attitudes will rub off on those we encounter and impact any environments where we are.

Gratitude Ignites Joy Flames

Gratitude is the entry way to joy. Grace brings contentment and trust. Expressing gratitude for God's provision ignites the flame. God delights in leaving handfuls of purpose. I Peter 1:8. These powerful moments build intimacy with Christ.

19

Following Christ gives our lives eternal meaning and purpose. Our world is full of people who see no meaning in life here on earth. Gratitude gives us a more potent witness as we invest our lives in eternity with Jesus. John 17:3, Luke 16:9.

Jesus gives us his blessing to spend our money extravagantly on things that show God's love. Galatians 6:8-10. Fight the good life of faith and faithfulness. Live that good life now. Do not wait until the future. John 17:2.

Joy transforms the ordinary. This involves mindfulness. Joy results when we stay in the present. The joy of the Lord then resides with us and our joy is complete. John 15:9-11. Joy binds us to Christ.

Sometimes when I write, I realize that God's fingerprints are on each page. When we choose to re-focus on the presence of God, the Spirit meets us there, transforming our ordinary days into sacred moments.

Joy empowers us. The power of joy comes despite the internal and external realities of our culture. Joy is never selfish. Joy is high-energy. Low energy disempowers. Our conscience creates reality. Like attracts like. When we feel joy, we tend to draw more joyful experiences.

Professor Chris Meadows has made the most comprehensive study of he phenomenology of the different forms of joy. When I took his class as part of my D.Div. study at Vanderbilt University, it resulted in my life ministry focus.

Meadows sorted through thousands of accounts of joy experiences from 333 university students. He concluded that there were three dimensions of the joy moment.

The first dimension is exited versus serene joy. Excited joy is very intense and involves high energy. Serene joy is quieter and calmer, giving feelings of harmony and unity. Meadows would agree that he positive valence of joy can range from intense powerful joy to less intense quiet delight.

Serene joy aims toward restoring the body to equilibrium. Excited joy is a sort of goal pursuit.

A second dimension he taught at Vanderbilt was individual and affiliative joy. Individual joy is experienced by an individual. Affiliative joy is joy that is shared with others.
Meadows discovered that 70 per cent of the experiences in his study were affiliative. Only 30 per cent were individual. The majority of instances of joy occur in affiliative or social settings. So, he concluded that joy is for social bonding.

A third dimension was anticipatory and consummatory joy. Anticipatory joy occurs when the fulfillment of a desire appears imminent. Consummatory joy happens when the desire has been fulfilled.

In this comprehensive study, Meadows identifies five phenom logical dimensions of joy.

The first is harmony and unity. This dimension involves a sense of internal harmony or integration within the self, and a sense of harmony with the other people including friends, family, nature.

The second one is called vitality. Excited joy involves increased vitality with energy, aliveness, and potency. The dimension of vitality activates appetitive systems that direct organisms to seek pleasure and reward.

The third one is transcendence. This describes the content of consciousness when a person senses or feels as she is moving or has moved or has passed away from normal existence. That person has transcended bounded space and time.

The fourth dimension is freedom. Freedom involves the experience of physical freedom. It also is the freedom of thought. Life is not fixed. Existence precedes thinking. To be, not to think, is how we know the joy of flowing into life. Thinking can think only about the known. It chews what is already chewed. To think is not to delve into anything original. We think because we know.

Joy is an experience, not a belief. Joy cannot appear by studying joy. Joy must be encountered and faced with surprise and freedom. God created us to be the original. We are free to be who we are. We cannot possibly become imitators. We will always be original.

Life is like a dance if we are all originals. Nobody is less than anybody else. Respect who you are and who God is. Respect your private inner voice and follow it.

Joy is like looking at a flower and becoming that flower. It is a dance around the flower. It is singing songs about the flower. Like a joy experience, the flower is dancing in the wind and singing alleluia and rejoice. Let the flower speak to your heart as Saint Francis of Assisi did, as he knew a taste of mystery. Francis dissolved himself in the dance. He became the dance.

Even saints commit many mistakes. They usually do not repeat the same mistake again. Listening to your own soul will move you in the right direction. Those discovering eternal joy will know the secret of listening to the spirit that dwells within you. Go where it takes you. Go where the joy is.

In our earthly journeys, we will all fail many times. We have the power in love and grace to rise again. The joy of the Lord helps us fall and rise again. Life goes on moving with uncertainties. That is life's freedom.

Each created person is a freedom, an unknown freedom. God gives us total freedom. If you understand what that choice means, we realize that insecurity is an intrinsic part of living. Life is freedom. Life is a continuing surprise.

We only have the present time. We never know what is going to happen. It's wonder as we wander.

Theologians and Bible scholars have drawn a tight connection between joy and physical freedom. In the story of David being overcome by his joy in the Lord that he leaps and dances in public. II Samuel 6:12-14. He doesn't notice that he is unclothed. Meadows described joy as altered perception. In a joy, people heightened awareness of depth, color, and touch. Sensations are brighter. More vivid. Clearer. Sharper. Calmer. Timeless.

To accept the challenge of the unknown takes faith. The experience of the joy that the unknown brings, ecstasy begins to happen. We need joy to become strong enough to keep a certain integrity. You think and feel that life is an adventure.

## Joy and Ecstasy

The limitation around joy needs to be drawn in the space between joy and ecstasy. As Meadows' transcendence of joy indicates, intense joy involves such a high degree of transcendence of the self, that a person loses the cognitive aspect of joy. Ecstasy wipes us out. Joy makes us intensely ourselves. Ecstasy appears as joy at or beyond its limitations. In some of my earlier books on the passion and the spirituality of joy, I contrast experiences of contentment, pleasure, satisfaction, and other things that ordinary people cannot discern from joy.

Chris Meadows wrote his Ph.D. dissertation at Princeton University.

> People in earthly power retain the power by disempowering other people. Religious and spiritual leaders and politicians spout platitudes about the worthy and the deserving, and those who are not.

As a joyologist and joy minister, I use my time and talent to find things that bring people joy. More than that, we must accept the power and positivity of joy. Letting ourselves feel joyful lets us feel empowered. With that strength, we spread that feeling to others.

Positive feelings dissolve negative feelings. We open space for positive feelings. Joy is the ultimate positive attitude. Feeling empowered creates incredible things. These things are capable of bringing us joy. Focus on now, not the past or future.

People worry about things that have yet to happen. We become anxious about our past and our visions of the future. Being present in the now allows more room for joy. When we feel positive energy and when we create from higher vibrations, we can create virtually anything.

Connecting to the joy of our soul is being present in the moment to nourish ourselves. The engaging involves being in the body and our creative energy. Opening our awareness of soul joy is the signal appearing as a subtle vibration, a gentle bubbling with an inner smile.
Connection brings more intuitive abilities, warmer relations with life, enjoyment, compassion, and gentleness. Lean into the joy. Enjoy unfiltered laughter. Bask in the joy. Milk those moments in your life for all they're worth.

Really enjoy your next meal. Like our French friends do, eat slowly. Be like Ina Garten, really taste the favors, and feel the food nourishing the body.

Play your favorite song of the moment. Listen or sing along, dance, lip sync, cry, and feel the music move through the body.

Hold somebody you love a bit longer than usual. The warmth of the touch will ignite a special connection.

Empowering ourselves and others makes people not only more resilient but more joyful, healthier, and creative. Consider what it means to elderly people unable to leave their homes as neighbors bring them groceries. We can go visit them wherever they live to share meaningful conversations that give them joy and new perspectives. To empower each other, people need to reflect on how they can spread a special purpose to strengthen communities.

Empowerment is the process of becoming stronger and capable of achieving more. The power of joy elevates communities and individuals. When individuals achieve this empowerment, they connect with those around them. They model what's possible. They inspire others to find their own paths.

This might include cheering ourselves up with some neat new clothes, a good dinner, a bouquet of flowers, as we share our lives with other people. Keep counting your blessings and giving thanks.
Joy is the cause, not the effect, of goodness in our lives. Joy increases with use, because we speak, think, and act with joy.

Sharing Knowledge

Knowledge transforms us in our vision quests and in change. Sharing knowledge brings people together. Sharing exposes us to different ways of thinking. We discover healthier eating habits, improved study habits, and efficiency in their physical workouts.

Sharing our individual stories takes courage. Doing so is liberating and empowering. Sharing our unique stories connects people and drives away loneliness. Hope comes as we are less isolated.

Listening to others with empathy and full attention provides them with an affirming experience. When people feel heard, they feel valued. Open communication fosters cooperative and collaborative relationships between people.

Sharing our knowledge yields more feedback and the ability to brainstorm situations or circumstances. The joy of Christ is contagious through human vestals like us. People will want to hang out with us. They will join our causes as well as those causes God expects us to stand in for those who are broken.

Standing Up for Others

Empowerment also means standing up for others. Speaking out against injustices supports our values and brings about equality to everyone. It protects entire neighborhoods from abuse or mistreatment.

People who are passionate about saving the planet can choose to become environmental justice workers.

Standing up for others means to offer positive words to someone who has received harsh treatment. Standing up in support lets people know that not everyone agrees with what happened. People can then be empowered to stand up for themselves.

Embrace positive thinking.

Norman Vincent Peale told us that positive thinking affects the mind, body, and soul. It was more than a catchphrase to Peale. Positive thinking boosts immunity, decreases stress, and increases the ability of analyze.

Positive thinking nurtures joy and positive moods. Our bodies release serotonin. We process information better. Positivity breeds positivity to give energy to keep on traveling forward even in these uncertain times.

Strong support helps us cope. It builds self-esteem. Drawing from the wellspring of joy, we cultivate new joy into our lives. God is the source of joy. Depend on our creator, the Source that never changes and from whom all goodness flows. Centering on the mind of Christ brings the power of joy.

In the final analysis, joy is an experience that no Christian can afford to miss. He discipline needed for joy is worth it. Joy will capture moments of celebration. Joy creates music in our souls. Growing as a Christian is to work on joy. One day our final destination will be not only entering heaven but entering into joy. Matthew 25:21.

Feeling the power of joy comes from the presence of Jesus Christ. Joy is a fruit of the Holy Spirit, the key to enjoyment in the Christian life.

Power comes by remaining in Christ, being attached to him, and abiding with him. Joy is not just an elective in being faithful to God. Philippians 4:4. We cannot afford to wait until circumstances settle down. Joy begins today. Joy begins with Jesus. Do not postpone your experiences of joy.

The apostle Paul's joy was related to his position in Christ, rather than his circumstances. The fountainhead of Paul's joy is not found anywhere in this world, but only in God.

Joy s fruit of the Spirit endures even during hardships, because it is developed from within us by the Holy Spirit. Paul recognized the need of the work of the Spirit. I Thessalonians 1:6.

Writing a book on joy, preaching joy to the world, teaching joy is what Peter referred to as "inexpressible and glorious." I Peter 1:8.

The joy of the Spirit is set apart from all levels of human joy. It is the result of faith in God. Romans 15:13. Jesus' followers are joyful people. No person remains the same as she was before the joy time of salvation. We commit our whole being to Jesus. We know Christ as savior and Lord. Luke 10:21. Jesus was full of joy through the Spirit. Psalm 45:7.
Christ praised his Father for the revelation of salvation. Jesus rejoiced that one lost sheep was found. Luke 15:5. Jesus spoke of joy when he bestowed his joy upon believers. John 15:11, 17:13. Human love flows out of human love. Joy loves people, life, and work. That same thing when the heavenly of the Spirit flows into our souls.

No love means no joy. Anything that breaks down love destroys joy. Human joy is not a lasting joy. The heavenly realm is not subject to change.

Powerful Acts of God

The Word of God contained in scripture is the revelation of God acting to restore humans to full and enjoying fellowship. God acted in the early church through the power of the Holy Spirit. Luke's gospel is commonly called the Acts of the Apostles. In all life situations, the joy associated with the indwelling spirit was a source of strength for rising above their circumstances. The question that Paul answers is the same as the rich young ruler asked in Luke 18:18-22.

28

We assume he was asking about eternal life after he dies. That is how I have interpreted these verses. Now, I cannot be sure, and I always consider how others see the words. It is interesting to read that story with the ideal of eternal life in mind.

The joy of the Lord is found in the assurance of salvation and the flowing of the Holy Spirit. Isaiah 61:10. The many blessings from God bring joy. Psalm 126:3.

Later in my book, I will write how joy hopes. Acts 24:5, Titus 2:13, Hebrews 6:19-20, Romans 5:2-5 are texts I used in sermons about hope. Our hope for future glory lies in hope. I Peter 1:3. We shall go from our imperfect life to eternal life in the presence of God.

I believe in the power of angels to enhance joy. Angels minister to us everywhere as God directs them. Psalm 34:7. In Acts 12:11, the apostle Peter shared that the Lord sent an angel to rescue Peter from prison. Angels rejoice when us sinners repent. Luke 15:10. The power of joy is the power over sin. The loving power of Jesus is with us in our present moments. When earthly trials arise, lean on Jesus, and we will discover his joy. Eternal life is both here and now. I Timothy 6:11-12. An old Nebraska farmer told me that one who lives only for today has the soul of a cow. Cows stay still all-day long munching on grass. They only think where the next mouthful will come.

The apostle Paul's words about life says we have the now we live in the present and eternal life while we are on our earthly journey very much on the present world. Romans 6:4, 6-13. If we are now living in eternal life, we must not allow sin to reign over us. Live the way God designed us to live, Paul would admonish. Jesus now has eternal life. And so do we. Eternal life will be extended after we die.

Everything Passes

29

Our sense of infiniteness becomes overwhelming. When my brother David died, on the front cover part of the funeral bulletin were the words, "Love is forever." As we reach our 80s and the ninth decade, we are so much more aware of the realities of living.

"It can attack us when we are staring at our children, or watching the leaves turn brown in the fall, or setting by a loved one in the hospital, or noticing how a neighborhood has run down, or realizing we are developing arthritis in our joints, or observing that the roses in a vase on the table have wilted since yesterday.

"It can creep over us when we look through an old photo album or stand behind an elderly person in the checkout line at the grocery store or find that your eyesight is getting worse for reading the telephone book, or see that the house needs painting again, or watch a familiar landmark being torn down to make way for something else or hear that someone has died." (John Killinger, *Letting God Bless You: The Beatitudes for Today*, p. 46)

Joy empowers!

# Chapter Two

# Joy Relates!

Joy is mostly experienced with loved ones. We feel emotionally safe when we feel deep love. When the object of our joy is long-lasting, people describe an intense feeling and a consuming positivity. Soften into joy.

Enjoy what enfolds.

We cherish family and friends, but we don't get to spend as much time with them as we desire. It is a person who energizes us. How many hours do you spend with them? Every day. Once a month. Once a year.

The simple conclusion is that close relationships create health. How can we nurture these relationships? Joy is based on giving ourselves. We relate to our beloved ones with no strings attached. A sense of kindness, fullness in our relating is the basis for joy. Time and attention are our greatest gifts.

Joy relates to people as they are now. Give up attempting to change another person. One of the biggest barriers to joy is our incessant desire to change another. This desire causes power struggles within relationships.

Finding joy in any relationship means having the ability to love unconditionally. The less we push, people can change themselves. We will delve into the art of listening in a later chapter. Joyous people listen. Listening is getting out of your own mind and being there wit the other person.

Stop that little voice inside your head and be quiet and available. When we really listen to another, we give up expectations of what we want to say or to be. Listening feels like being loved.

Being human, our life journey will bring regrets for some of our actions. I look at my daughter and grandson and I can't help but wonder how they have grown into such fine adults.

I made many mistakes. There are hurts in their lives, some of which I am not even aware. Surely the grace of God has been with my family for generations.

My thoughts and dreams turn more and more in relationships with my old friends and family members. God turns my mistakes into life lessons. Everyone of us regret our failures of various kinds, our missed opportunities, and the things that could have been, and so many dreams unfulfilled.

We have within our genes, the good and bad, My McReynolds family descended from Robert the Bruce in Scotland. The majority of our family history shows we are related to John McReynolds (1665-1760) of County Tyrone in Northern Ireland. My sixth great grandfather, James McReynolds (1742-1809) was a talented and busy man who lived in Virginia. As for his moral honesty, it was frequently said, "As honest as James McReynolds."

Most of them were spiritual and belonged to the Presbyterian church. They fought in the American Revolution with a Virginia militia. The McReynolds clan aligned themselves mainly with the Confederate States during the American Civil War, from 1861-1865. (Billy Kennedy, *The Scots-Irish in the Shenandoah Valley*, chapter 19, "The pioneering McReynolds from County Tyrone," pp. 153-158)

As I learn more about my descendants, I am indebted to them for what good there is in me. Human beings do the best

32

they can with what they have, where they are planted, when they lived, and how they react to others for the joy of the Lord, which shall not be complete until God prepares us to relate in the heavenly kingdom.

It is time to forgive the erring parent, embrace the estranged sibling, let go of disappointments in a prodigal child." (Gail Sheehey, *New Passages*, p. 142)

The apostle Paul expressed his regret for his days as Paul. Philippians 3:13-14. Paul did not repeat the same unhealthy relational patterns in his past.

Joy occurs within relationships. Communication is the foundation. Respect, honesty, compassion, and humor are important. A sign of joy is that human beings feel comfortable communicating openly and honestly. They enjoy spending time together. The companionship is genuine. There is mutual respect for each other's opinions and thoughts.

People who relate as married couples want to feel loved and appreciated. Small gestures of affection go a long way as people relate to one another. Joy comes as we support each other. Discover ways that connect like snuggling up on the sofa together. Make joy a priority to relate what brings joy.

Joy relates with God.

"Man's chief end is to glorify God and enjoy God forever" are words from the Westminster catechism. Joy relates to God, not as an end in itself. As a verb joy enjoys. Joy is a spontaneous human relationship found in God through Christ. John 16:22-24, 17:13.

Joy is an unshakable position of power and strength in God. Nehemiah 8:10. Joy is bound to Christian sanctification as an integral part of the fruit of the Holy Spirit. Love, joy, peace, patience, kindness, goodness, faithfulness, gentleness, and self-control. Galatians 5:22. The chief end of humankind is to enjoy joy. All joy longs for God.

This book will focus on the power of joy to transform lives and bring about humankind's flourishing as we come alive for a new tomorrow in our world. My vision is that joy is our destination. Flourishing and joy are synonymous. Life is a journey and our earth trip ill be much richer if our path contains more joys. Joy is a positive emotion. Joy has been used with differing meanings. The word "positive" is derived from the past participle of the Latin language *pono* and p*onere* meaning as verbs as making something present. From Roman times, the word positive denoted optimism or preferred, desired, or filled with goodness. Writers in our day focus on positive thinking or the new positive psychology that integrates with joy.

What We Want Determines Joy.

We have goals in life and goals with God. These goals tell us much about the level of joy that we are experiencing. We seek to be close to God. Being close to God produces joy. Ecclesiastes 2:1-11, Psalm 22:26,27:4- 5, 119:1-2.

Finding God is completely relational. The more God knows the real and authentic you, the closer you feel to he joy of God. The more and harder we search and seek for God to understand who God is, feels, and wants, the more we are drawn. We desire to feel a certain way in our life journey.

Our closeness to God determines our joy. Take time to pray about what you appreciate about God. Not just what God has given, but who God is. Job 20:4-5, Nehemiah 8:12, Psalm 1:1-3, 9:2, 34:5, 63:4-5, 90:14.

Joy relates! My wife Laurel does more to relate joy in her life than anyone I have ever known. As I write, she is making about six pies for what is called a pie ride. She frequently asks people to come enjoy a delicious meal that she has created.

People are seated around the tables or anywhere they find a place. Children run around in our new home. Some build things with Legos. Some play cars and trucks. If a child breaks something, we never hear one peep from Laurel.

God made us for community and connection. The joy we share deepens our connection and stimulates us and joy increases.

I have about 250 scrapbooks with walls of faces of those who brought joy into my life. Naming does not merely give a caption for a photograph. It allows a narrative of my past and present life to be played out in my mind. I often take time to review the external and internal of what occurred. My own family and friends look so young and fresh, as we have all grown older.

I cherish all these relationships with folks I have encountered throughout the world. My collection adds motivation, emotion, and the enjoyment of a life lived in the midst of the joy of the lives of others.

## The Relationship to Relationships

Healthy relationships are characterized by interdependence with loved ones. We shares ourselves without losing ourselves. We mutually depend on each other.

Our relationship with relationships become joyless if you struggle to trust. We fear being vulnerable. We feel our children's emotions too deeply. We blame others instead of taking ownership in relationships. We fear having conflict. We fear being abandoned or disappointed that results in a lack of boundaries and lack of self-care.

Relationships are worth the risk. We need people in our lives. We seek to be part of an engaged community who know us. God created us with a desire to belong. "Emotional connection is a sign of mental health. It is emotional isolation that is the killer." (Sue Johnson, *Love Sense: The Revolutionary New Science of Romantic Relationships,* p. 22)

Needs are not met by someone else. Human relationships sometimes will bring on disappointment. We are created to be in relationship with God. The creator designed us to need a variety of relationships, calling us to love God first and our neighbor as ourselves. We need to love all three.

## Failure and Relationships

Failure is necessary in relationships. We attempt to avoid any conflict, so we relate in shallow ways. We all fail in relationships, because none of us are perfect.

Repairing relationships is a needed skill. We can learn to communicate through tough issues and then draw even closer. (R.F. Baumeister and M.R. Leary, "The Need to Belong: Desire for Interpersonal Attachments as a Fundamental Human Motivation," *Psychological Bulletin*, pp. 497- 529)

Naming and taking in events gives me a sense of order. Recollection comes when I carefully arrange my photographs in an album. I give meaning to each one by ordering them according to time, place, and the celebration of family and ministry events. I have formed a lasting collection.

My collections have a dominant theme that tells my life story. My faith and faithfulness increases as I name the moments in which God appeared and rescued me with a permanent sense of meaning.

Recollection is like arranging photos in an album. Rather than merely sticking pictures randomly, my valued collections give meaning to each one by arranging them according to the event, the persons in each photo, and the time and date.

I do not know if God has anything such as movies, photographs, or media that records our journeys. God is always relating a story. My Creator has been involved in the passing minutes of every one of my days and every single day of my life.

God is both the narrator and writer as we become aware, enthralled, and participated in the wonderous story of God.

Joy relates!

# Chapter Three

# Joy Feels!

Recall the last time you experienced joy. Remember how it felt. Joy feels like excitement, amazement, or trilling. Joy has its own biological signatures. We feel joy in our entire body. Joy moves us so quickly that a cascade of other human experiences show up. Wonder. Delight. Surprise. Flow.

Mindful awareness or being in the moment brings more joy experiences. Explore the beliefs that motivate behavioral choices. Change the way we talk to ourselves. Reflect on beliefs all the time. Things we tell ourselves move us closer to the possibilities of joy, or further away. Follow your bliss.

Joy may be fleeting. It leads to gratitude for the moment of time. Joy is likely felt during the birth of a child, graduations, major achievements, or publishing a new book.

Joy involves changing the way we engage in the world. Colors appear brighter. Physical movements feel freer and easier, and smiling involuntarily happens. Our thinking and attention opens up to creativity and the ability to solve complex problems. Joy feels light and bright, playful and empowering. Joy fills our soul. Our foreheads feel calm. Our eyebrows become motionless and arched. The corners of the mouth are raised. The complexion is bright. The cheeks are ruddy. I find it difficult to know how the expression of joy appears in our bodies from simple or momentary glimpses.

This feeling is more intense with loved ones. It feels emotionally safe. The feeling of joy relies on subjective and individual interpretation. Joy feels positive and good, and in a joy, people dance, clap, or jump for joy. Celebration time!

Joy enables knowing what is important. In a joy, you desire more joy. Joy is felt when you see somebody you really like. Joy relates socially. Expressing joy makes people around us igniting increase in intense connections.

## Lightness in Our Bodies

Joy feels like lightness in your body. Time seems to fly by quickly. We feel warmer. We sense the energy. We feel more *joie de vivre*. We were introduced to cranberry spritzers in France. It is simply cranberry juice and seltzer water. Now when we share with friends, we make them more festive by serving them in a wine glass with a sprig of fresh mint. This treat becomes more elegant and enjoyable.

Our French friends have taught us that a cup of tea tastes better in a porcelain cup. We, like the French and English, can experience our own version of high tea.

Janet Ruth Gendler, a native of Omaha, give fresh expression to the feeling of sensuality. She wrote, "Sensuality does not wear a watch but she always gets to he essential places on time. She is adventurous and not particularly quiet. Sensuality has exquisite skin and she appreciates it in others as well. There are other people whose skin is soft and clear and healthy, but something about Sensuality's skin announces that she is alive. When the sun bursts forth in May, Sensuality enjoys taking off her shirt and feel the sweet warmth of the sun brush across her shoulder. This is not intended as a provocative gesture.

"Sensuality does not understand why everyone is disturbed by her. She makes love at the borders where time and space change places. Sensuality is in love these days. Her new friend is sweet. Climbing into bed for the first time, she confessed he was intimidated about making love with her. Sensuality laughed and said, 'We have been making love for days.'" (Janet Ruth Gendler, *The Book of Qualities*, pp. 96-97)

Harmony, unity in personal integration, creativity, and new insight come from joy. Joy presupposes love. Love gives a rise to desire which draws lovers in their uniting and harmony. Delight and joy arise from desires fulfilled. The French word *jouissance* connotes sensual and bodily desire and satisfaction.

The most powerful touches we encounter are not planned and arrive unrehearsed. We discover an opening to life with the flow of the Spirit. We are opened and embraced as our being touched causes us to feel a quiet quiver. The life of God within is awakened by the spiritual touch. Just as physical touch incites the experience of the human journey, spiritual touches open our awareness of the divine world. The sense of touch never wears off.

Long lasting joy feels like a sense of going with the flow. We feel animated and alive, positive and good. (Larry Cottrell, "Joy and Happiness: A Simultaneous and Evolutionary Concept," *Journal of Advanced Nursing*, pp.1506-1517.

Unlike erotic feelings that look simply for the pleasure of the lovers as a means to an end. To gain pleasure is different from the concepts of Jesus. To love someone is not using them. Memory will provide "a union of likeness." There is an awareness and hope of maintaining joy when the beloved one has gone away.

When you share your story, tell folks the difference in your thinking about God's gift of sexuality before and after Jesus transformed you.

Sexual Feelings

We associate joyous relationships with quality sex. Joy feels in the affection that accompanies sexuality. Kissing, hugging, and touching two adoring people contributes to relationship satisfaction and well-being. Couples are more likely to enjoy sex more often because the feelings satisfy. Joyful people who are more positive get involved in love relationships that benefits their well-being.

The impact of sex on joy is accounted for by increases of affection inked to prior sexual activity. Sex predicts affection. Affection predicts sexual activity. Sex is beneficial because of its physiological effects that promote a stronger and positive connection.

Some speakers and writers declare joy to be a spiritual emotion. These people do not associate joy with physical sensations of pleasure. Joy is enhanced where there is a spiritual dimension to the experience. One is more likely to experience joy in a sexual encounter when one see the transcendentness of the interaction.

When a person enjoys wine, as the French do, she sees the wine as a divine blessing. Joy feels! This feeling is enhanced when there is a divine purpose. If joy is so important for a flourishing life, then we are encouraged to advance our understanding of joy.

We cannot understand human beings unless we understand joy and how this feeling comes to be. Understanding joy is crucial to grasp human flourishing. Yet, it is the least studied human emotion. Evidence supports the theory that joy is a specific emotion and a distinct positive emotion.

Joy and Moods

Joy differs from moods. Joy is always about something perceived as good in one's journey. Joy is a response to a positive, good object. Joy is unique in that when someone receives good news, we wonder what makes news good. It is news that we have been waiting for and it gives hope. If one feels they are favored, joy is the probable consequence.

When one person draws emotional benefits from sex, the relationship satisfaction is also promoted and deeply felt. Working on their physical affection toward each other stirs up a reestablished joy. The Holy Spirit prevents the soul from being distracted by external circumstances and the turmoil of losing someone whom you loved. Divine joy keeps relationships within boundaries and with a healthy orientation to the reality of now. God loves us. God enables us to love in return. Joy feels! Ina most loving relationship, joy is always imperfect. We look forward to the day when joy lasts forever and is complete and perfect. There will be nothing left to desire. I Corinthians 2:9.

We will be given life through the grace of God in Jesus. We shall enjoy God's joy and rest. Humans are inseparable from God's destiny for us. Psalm 96:11-13.

The hidden face of God will become a shining face. Psalm 30:11, 51:8-12. God will be singing in joy with the redeemed. Zephaniah 3:17. Eternal life comes as our earthly life is taken up by our joyous God with our heavenly life which is forever. Luke 15:7-10.

In my previous book on the spiritual meanings and goodness of sexuality was a refute to churches and church leaders' negative and damaging words and practices of sexuality. My book is listed in the biography.

Sex is really about God and our deep desire that we feel for God. Human sexuality is an analogous relationship to divine desire. Sex brings potential for pleasure. Pleasure in woven into our sexual response.

Sexual pleasure is an important part of faith. Love, spirituality, and sexuality are bound together. God created human beings who practice sex in the full sense of the word. Genesis 1:31.

Contrary to the belief of many Christians, the writers of Holy Scripture were not as concerned about acts of sexual intercourse as they were about human relationships. Jesus made love the central core of his message. Nowhere in his teaching does he condemn sexual pleasure. He taught wholeness, spiritual well-being, and loving relationships.

Our experience with God involves the feelings in our entire body. Joy feels! So what comes first, he emotion or the body's response? Our feelings and our physical bodies are inextricably linked. When we experience joy, the emotional and physical response happens instantly.

Joy feels! When it does, we get the urge to jump for joy. Even the act of smiling helps. Our breathe picks up when we are doing something that is an enjoyment for us. That breath of life slows down when we are doing a relaxing pleasurable activity such as a slow walk in a park.

Pupils in our eyes dilate when we are aroused sexually. They shrink or grow based on our emotional state. Notice that when you are in a joy, the face flushes and your heart races.

Our circulatory system consists of our hearts, the veins, blood vessels, lymph, and blood.

Joy is the most acknowledged divine potential in us. Jesus expressed his dream in the words of Isaiah Luke 4:18-19. Let joy reveal our potential that has been hiding inside. Every person experience feelings of joy.

Joy comes with a new love. The birth of a child oozes out joy. Completion of a new book. Joy is the feeling with success of a loved one. The joy of recognizing the gift of someone who expressed a similar feeling of love for me.

Every moment we are present to life, joy has a better chance of surprising us. Do not postpone joy. You might just miss it.

To sustain a vision of joy is never easy. Consider the parable of the Sower. Mark 4:16-17. The feeling of joy is expandable, scary, and vulnerable. Be joyful because the Good News has arrived. These words from Jesus are especially suitable to our modern times. God designed our whole beings for joy. The fairy tales that we read to our kids put it in these words, "They lived happily ever after." Our seminary professors put it another way: "We are made for eternal living." (Robert T. Sears, "A Theology of Joy and Healing," *The Journal of Christian Healing*, pp. 3-22)

Biblical joy does not depend on the mere feeling. It is about building right relationships. Proverbs 3:4, Luke 2:52. We no longer have to search for security. Some call joy a feeling or a positive emotion. As a spiritual sensation of the depositing of the joy of Christ into the soul, to live there forever.

Joy brings us a proper response to a hurting world. The joy of Christ in us is beyond anything in this earthly place. If joy of the Lord is our life foundation, the walls we live in will be stable. Joy keeps us grounded and secure.

If we have joy in our lives as seen by the people around us, it is because of our firm belief flows through us. If a person feels no joy, the belief and surrender to Christ is just not there.
The concepts which Jesus asks us to believe produce the fruit of the Spirit in our lives The fruit including joy is meant for others to taste.

Fruit starts within the vine, unseen before it emerges. If it isn't stirred within, the fruit will not mature and ripen on the branches of our lives for others to taste and feel. We believe in our hearts just what the Holy Spirit believes.

Our goal is to become more like Jesus. We must act, think, and feel like Jesus. To be in joyful radiance, we must practice spiritual life in Christ consistently. Real transformation happens. We will become more joyful than we were a year before. This joy is repeated during all the years of our lifetime.

The joy of the Lord makes us positive people for others. We will want to be like Jesus, because we belong to Jesus. II Corinthians 5:17. The building of the kingdom of joy requires faith and faithfulness and Christ is now inviting us to participate. We must embrace the vision of Jesus for our lives. Jesus wants us to be like him. Jesus is inviting us to start living this new way of life in the present now time.

I feel Christ stirring within me so I can become like him. I want to feel more and more joy. II Peter 1:5-11.

Joy feels!

# Chapter Four

# Joy Fulfills!

Envision your precious life. When I sit down in my home office to write, it's because a story or a simple quote runs through my mind as a catalyst for a sermon or a book.

Darkness and despair are not the final truth. We endure by turning to joy and fulfillment. French philosopher Jean-Paul Sartre said, "Life begins on the far side of despair." Sartre discovered glimpses the light thru the darkness. Beyond the darkness, we find joy and fulfillment.

We try to repress and submerge the dark despair with activities. This is the human attempt. This keeps us from being aware of ourselves at deepest levels. Busyness leaves us spiritless and joyless.

Any joy we experience will be diminished. Joyless people care deeply about certain things and they are susceptible to intense joy. I witness the euphoria that swept Louisiana State University baseball fans when their team won the 2023 College World Series in Omaha.

That euphoric demonstration of fulfillment was short lived. People had already forgotten that Ole Miss and Mississippi State had won in the previous two years. Those two teams were not in it in college NCAA tournament 2023.

Stanford and Wake Forest players and fans actually cried tears of disappointment for not winning the prize. Wake Forest had not been in Omaha since 1955. Few Wake Forest people were being sustained by the joy they felt back in 1955.

Fulfilling their team's goal for the seventh time in Omaha, LSU's joy was nothing like the joy that sustained Paul through his many tribulations. Joy is often precarious in a way that our joy in God is not precarious. Joy is important for our inner fulfillment.

## Turning toward Joy

In our life journey, we began life as infants. Like a newborn learning how to use its hands and feet, we fumble around in spirit, groping in the dark seeking release. During our struggle, a door opens. We turn toward the light to find another glimpse. We feel new inner joy. We know that we are full of joy. This joy does not depend on our circumstances. Solid, given, and inexplicable joy comes in the midst of despair, misery, and suffering.

Our life journey has a beginning and an end. Life flies by quickly. Considering the average number of weeks we live. Most of us live about 4,000 weeks. Every person has the same 24 hours in one day. Time wasted is time gone forever.

If we feel unhappy, we blame outside things like our past, our parents, the lack of opportunities, our health, we are the only one who can change it. Life is controlled by ourselves.

The impossible becomes possible, only if you believe it. If we do not believe, we must shift things and begin living, nothing will happen. Expect that. Accept that. Life is like a staircase, sometimes we will go up, and sometimes we go down.

Most of us can cite our many failures. Failure is a part in our roads to success. Failure gives us feedback. Make adjustments. Move forward. Our journey towards life is life. We will have our ups and downs. Sitting around waiting for life to change is not the way to achieve your life calling. We dream big dreams but we place them on a shelf.

# Keep Doing What You Are Doing

If we keep on doing what we are doing now, we will keep on getting what we are now getting. Shift how you feel. What's going on in your life right now really matters.
No life is perfect. Nobody can bone up to what we expect of them. Some people spend their precious time waiting. People wait for new relationships, a new job, building a new home, buying a new automobile going on a vacation.

Nobody knows what anyone's future will be like. Waiting for another time in the future we think will be better. Face it. Once we obtain those things, and once we achieve amazing things, then we will live with joy.

Joy is the pearl of great price. We open our souls and joy comes. Joy fulfills against the background of ordinary fulfillment. When I finish another book, I feel a sense of fulfillment. This means a longing has been satisfied.

Turning toward joy is something like landing an airplane after dark, in a dense fog. Like an aircraft pilot, we have no clear visual clues. We ride down on a radio beam. Our locator signal indicates that we are on the correct path.

We move from beyond tuning out and covering up our blindness and despair. Our security blankets are kept under wraps. Joy is not desensitization but being fully alive.

Fulfilling joy releases us from tension, striving, need for success or fame, recognition, and achievement. These are the characteristics involved in attempting to fulfill ourselves. We retune our souls t become fully and consistently living in joy.

Joy fulfills so we don't work our entire lives only to discover that we never focused on what we wanted. Being fulfilled gives us contentment and joy in our journeys.

Jesus Christ is the source of human life and the universe. Fulfillment means living a good life socially and individually. Joy fulfills human purpose. Attention to human fulfillment in relation to Christ is revealed in the teaching and witnessing of martyrs, Origen and writings of the early fathers, and in the monastic movement. I refer to he early "fathers," because each of them were male. Most of them were church bishops.

Jesus accomplished complete human fulfillment. Other human beings flourish by participating in Christ's divine-human life. As the early rules of faith and the Nicene Creed pronounce, Jesus was a single reference. He is the divine son of God who became human, died and rose for our sins. Jesus will return to judge the living and the dead. He will reign forever at the right hand of God the Father.

We will joyfully know that I am I, a person standing beyond ourselves. Our physical existence is found in our genes. These genes began to form our bodies soon after conception.

On the day we were born, social conditioning began to shape our being. Human striving is expressed more deeply in our quest for love. Our highest desire is to love and be loved, to care for others, and for others to care about us. Most believe that romantic love is a learned response unleashed in surprise.

Joy relates!

Words characterize the mind with human language. Hand signs replace words. We think in metaphors, the ability to transport an insight from one experience to another. Living joy in our minds is made up of talking, thinking, writing, reading, and relating to those surrounding us in the present time, and those ancestors who were on their life journeys generations ago.

There really is no future. There will be no new past. We must live now. When the future arrives, it will come in the now.

## Jesus and Flourishing

Jesus told his disciples to be faithful, not to flourish. A grain of wheat must fall into the ground and die. John 12:24. Christians learn about fulfillment from the story of Jesus and his incarnation and atonement. Love is a necessary condition for realizing human values. I Corinthians 13:1-3. Virtues lead to human flourishing.

Jesus taught us that human fulfillment lies in unconditional love. By communicating his Spirit to the world, Christ empowers unconditional love. Human fulfillment is the effect of love. It is not love's inspiration, justification, or motive.

Jesus displayed what love means in concrete words. The living Christ brought the communication of the Holy Spirit into the world. By God's love and grace, the Spirit is present to every human being.

God is love. God is good. God's desire is for us to be fulfilled and to flourish. Christ is the pathway to joy.

Our behaviors and actions leave a lasting memory on others, painting an accurate picture of you as you want to be remembered. What is the meaning and purpose of your life? Consider your personal beliefs, your values, and your dreams and goals.

Life is an unwinding road. Filled with bumps and curves, we buckle under living pressure which is a frustrating place. Material possessions, jobs, other people and wealth do not fulfill. Sinking into a deep pit of despair, these things have let them down.

Life is a journey that takes us to different individual destinations. We are responsible to enjoy life to its fullest. Living a life of joy and fulfillment is by choice. We have the power to make that decision for ourselves.

Becoming immune to our situations irrespective of the outcomes is how we create joy. We need to reflect on our current state in life. We become too overwhelmed with the pressures of life. Ask yourself, "Where am I and where am I headed?" We must be contented wherever we are placed. Reflect on where you are at this moment.

Don't be so frustrated by the things you have no control over. This is the reality of life. We are not given control. Let it go. Believe the best. Believe that anything is possible. Keep your distance from the naysayers who drown our energy. Some people destroy our hope. Three will be light at the end of the tunnel. Keep on being positive. Allow that kind of environment to see you through life's journey.

Breathe and be thankful for the little things. Feeling blue about all your disappointments will bring you incessant frustrations. Don't be just concerned about life's bigger things. If we focus there, we forget and never gain a life of joy.

Saying something should not be this way will not change our situation. This now is your life. It's not the situation that is causing negative feelings. Our thoughts about the situation cause those negative and useless feelings.

If you dear reader, continue doing what you are doing, complaining staying unhappy. Days, weeks, months, and years will pass you, and your life will never become different or better.

I love God. I enjoy what I am doing now. I reach millions worldwide, helping people bounce back from difficult times. How much time do I have left? Nobody knows.

As the noted Alcoholics Anonymous prayer says "change the things you can. We are just lazy folks. We do nothing. There are a few areas in life where we have a little bit of control.

The experience of a joyful life depends on the efforts we put in ourselves. Every human being born on earth is uniquely gifted. We just don't have the patience to discover our potential that God has endowed us with. As long as there is life, joy will hope us into fulfilling lives.

Turning up the volume on all the noise in our lives, we deeply appreciate silent and still moments. We become more grounded and relaxed.

We might not need the things that we think we need. Cease the lack thinking. Abundant, fulfilling life is now before our eyes. Slow down and look Lack can be transformed into more and better tastes, better sights, warmer touches, heavenly smells. Everything thing becomes a sensual delight.

People who worry too much, plan for every possible outcome in each situation. If we do not love ourselves, we try to make everything perfect. Seeing the world in terms of problems is clearly flawed. Giving up the effort to change ourselves or anybody else.

There is always space for the flow of further experiences. Focusing on our present problems keeps us from taking stock of what is working in your life.

If some grudge is interfering with your joy, give this your attention. Live in forgiveness. Making a lifestyle of living free from grudges gives us empowerment with strong, clear, and pure feelings.

Learn from the challenges of your life. Be honest about your buttons that are pushed. Difficulties can show us the areas of life that we continue to work on. No matter how difficult your life is, you can show up in a good- natured, smiling, and opening. Be kind and agreeable.

Every moment offers a choice. Reflect on your life and how joy is the barometer for finding the way through life. Try an alternate path. If today was your last, what would you do. Today. Only today. Commit to joy. Exchange non-joy moments with joy. Add and replace. See your patterns. Go from resistance to seeking.

Become the best version of yourself. Show up for the world in a more loving, joyful way. Time id now ticking Think about how many weeks you have left. The time is now. It's time to surrender to God and make things happen.

Jesus is never impressed by moral blamelessness but by honest openness. Our spiritual sense tells us that the meaning of our lives lies outside of us. It is in the Mystery that creates us. To be fully human, even in the midst of oppression, we must look beyond ourselves to our relationship with God. Mark 1:15

Our goal and mission is to have God through Jesus Christ and the Holy Spirit to reign in us. Others, including those being freed from human oppression are attracted to Jesus and those who live in joy. To do so, we must step out of the box. Remember God created you as an original. Get out of that worldly box. Be free from human oppression. Stretch yourself. Think. Choose. Dream big.

## Liberation from Human Oppression

To some, Christ is the one who saves souls. Jesus is the compassionate prophet. He said love comes in that unconditional love of our neighbor. Matthew 25:40.

God wants us to flourish in every way possible. Grace enters every area of human existence. Incomprehensible love is revealed in the resurrection. Resurrection includes the whole human person, body and soul.

Human flourishing is moral, material, and eternal. Luke 4:4. Human flourishing on earth and in heaven is rooted in love of neighbor and God. Jesus shows us this love. John 14:6. Love is not only a sacred sphere but exists in every part of life. Joy is the effect of love. This love is the foundation for the goodness of creation and friendship with our community.
Jesus came in the form of a servant, a slave. He loved both friends and enemies. His divine grace empowers our transformation. Love reveals the fullness of God. Love of God is the summary of free fulfillment. The New Testament proclaims a new creation, a new wine, a new earth, and a new heaven. (Werner Jeanrond, *A Theology of Love*, p. 143)

Human flourishing depends on the love and grace of God. Divine grace is also the grace of Christ. Grace of Christ is the essential for human flourishing. To love God is to believe in love.

Jesus is able to assume human form and blend it with himself in his divine nature, because of his divine identity. Christ's incarnation is God's human action and passion for our salvation. Christ's divinity is evident in the divine statements from the Bible.

The purpose of the incarnation was for the Son of God to undergo a human death for our salvation. The incarnation of the divine son leads to the full, natural functioning of human nature for the first and only time.

Jesus Christ had a complete and fully functioning human mind. He had his own will. Christ is a complete human being. He possessed self- determination and human choice.

The biblical accounts make both divine and human statements about Jesus. Scripture also makes divine statements about the human Jesus.

Store the Joyful Moments

Store joyful moments. Go beyond your mind. Be freely aware. Overthinking is a vicious cycle. Joy is spiritual work. Joy is growth. Connection. Success. Well-being. Fulfillment.

Joyful moments are stored in our life tapes. Experiencing joy makes ordinary moments extraordinary with exponential value. Looking outside my office window, I saw a mother with her four- or five-year-old daughter. They stood next to a tree. He child was watching some of the many squirrels. The daughter stepped toward the squirrels. They ran up into the tree They stopped halfway up the trunk looking back to her. The little girl burst out in laughter.

In those tapes stored in my brain contain many joy filled times when my own little girl was laughing. Joy was connected those moments stored in my head. Wonderful moments. Special moments. Joy!

Recall a moment in time when you experienced joy. Maybe it was when your child was born. Maybe when you finally made a team. Perhaps the joy of receiving an appointment or call to become pastor of a church congregation.

C.S. Lewis said, "Joy is the serious business of heaven." Joy is also the serious business of earth. God fulfills us with joy. Fulfilling joy! Amazing gift. Joy makes our lives richer and it brings emptiness without it. Fulfilling joy is complex. Once you've experienced it, you want to experience it again and again.

Imagine living in a space hat makes it easy to find joy. Put on a song that brings a smile. When we understand that joy is abundant, we will most likely find opportunities to make it so.

Joy is a deep gladness. Contentment. Delight. Joy is like a river that never ceases to flow. Joy runs deeper than pleasure or pain. Scripture informs us that joy comes in the midst of difficult circumstances.

It was in a dangerous moment that Jesus spoke to his disciples in the upper room the night before his death. It took them by surprise, as joy often does. John 15. In this scripture, we see that the love of God in Christ and the joy of Jesus are tied together. Abiding in Christ, living in the will of God are linked together in joy.

No matter how enriching our past memories may be, these are now gone. Be fulfilled today. Psalm 118:34. This is the date for rejoicing. Look through your old photographs or pictures in your cell phone. Delight in the people God has placed into your life. Rejoice in the experiences you have been privileged to enjoy.

Our obedience to Jesus and the experience of his joy comes with this heavenly delight. God wants to give the intimacy with him in the fullness of his grace. Living in a way contrary to what the Bible teaches, we should not be surprised when we lack joy.

Joy is the indication that what we are made of is being fulfilled. Being in tune with God brings joy. Joy comes when we are touched by love. Joy is a commitment. Hebrews 12:2. Joy is grounded in the total, self-giving love from God. One of my favorite verses in Nehemiah is "The joy of the Lord is my strength." We exist in the image of God. If God is joyful, ten to be joyful is to become like God. God rejoices in us. We actually share God's being. As a mother delights in her child, bone of her bone, so God delights in us.

Young people have spoken about "free love." They think that they are not bound and are free to enter into any relationship. Commitment frees us to celebrate and play.

Joy is a passion. When I was fitted for hearing aids, I heard the singing of birds for the first time. As Saint Francis discovered, even the birds responded to his preaching. Joy in Christianity is only found in Jesus. John 15:7-8.

God never lets go of the divine dream. It is grounded in the image in the heart and soul of every human being. Already as e read in Genesis, God took steps to restore the dream. God sent Jesus to fulfill the dream. Christ said yes to all God promised. II Corinthians 1:18-20,

Jesus is the one whose whole being is in intimate relationship with God. His faithfulness unto death is what fulfilled the dream of God.

## Abiding in Faith Fulfills God's Dream and Ours

Count it all joy. James 1:2-4. Joy is strengthened by the experiences we go through to bring it into reality. We become the salt for earth, and the light of the world. Jesus tells us to enter the narrow gate. He also said, "Those who hear and carry out my words are building on a solid rock."

We contemplate God's joy so we can model our lives on God. Luke 3:16, Matthew 5:48, John 17:4. As we listen and carry out the things we hear, we will experience the generous love of God and be grounded in joy. The passionate love of God is infinitely creative and community building. Love is not complete until it is shared. The Holy Spirit is the shared love of the Father and the Son. The early Christian community was known for its sharing. Sharing made God's love complete. I John 1:3-4. With our faithfulness and sharing, our joy is complete.

This fulfillment results in the perception that a person's life is being well- lived. (Philip Watkins, Robert Emmons, and Joshua Bell. *The Journal of Positive Psychology*, pp. 1-99)
If you desire to cultivate more joy and love into your life. Connect yourself to a higher vision for life. Joy is a glimpse of eternal reality. Moments of joy will knit together. Little by little, like a mosaic, fragments of grace will merge to form a complete picture.

God has a divine plan unfolding at the level of our soul. Because every event in your life happens affects the person's soul. Deeply connect to discover the power of joy for your journey. (Sandy Roman, *Living with Joy: Keys to Personal Power and Spiritual Transformation*, pp. 30-44)

# Chapter Five

# Joy Listens!

Recently, I purchased hearing aids. I hear so much that I never heard before. What joy to hear birds sing, pages of a book crinkle, sounds of my typing on my computer and the sounds of my printer. Someone said, "God gave us two ears and one mouth."

My wife would say:" Jim, you might be hearing me, but are you listening?" Hearing and l listening are two different things. Listening involves actively paying attention to words and sounds that you hear to realize their meaning. Joy listens! If we choose not to listen to our spouse, co-workers, friends, or children, we create a riff in these relationships.

Hearing new sounds was a blessing as I now hear with hearing aids. To master communication and hearing is required to become successful in our precious relationships. Listening and hearing are essential for our life journeys.

Imagine what happens if every time you listened to someone, you were aware that the words were wrappings around feelings. This is joyful listening. Listening requires concentration and effort. Only in silence can we touch souls. People will know they are heard and acknowledged. Our souls need to have ears and eyes for feelings. Communication is not only about us.

Interruptions while someone is talking is not listening. Interrupting means we are not listening. We cannot wait for the gap in the conversation before we react to the messege we think we heard.

Hearing is a passive act having to do with sound. Hearing is how we collect data. Every day, all day, we hear sounds and words.

Listening revolves around actively paying attention to the words and sounds to develop an emotional response. We can hear words and sounds without listening. Active listening requires curiosity, purpose, motivation, and effort. Joy listens! Joy attempts to understand what is heard to make a connection.

Passive listening is listening that is disconnected, inattentive, and unreceptive. There is no effort to contribute to conversations.

Imagine you are listening to God when you listen to others. This will transform the communication. It only takes a spark to get a fire glowing. The spark of the Divine lives in every child of God. To listen and to speak to that part of God in everyone is wisdom. Remember that every conversation we have is with God, no matter to whom you are now speaking.

Listening transforms relationships.

Listening can be a creative force. It has the power to transform relationships. Listening brings awareness that we are present with each other and with God.

Hearing and listening Affects our mental health. When we choose not to listen to our spouse, colleagues, peers, friends, or children, we experience a lacking in our mental health.

The joy of hearing and listening creates strong and warm relationships. We can understand and exchange knowledge. We can share our memories. We will much better solve conflicts and come up more effective solutions.

We will better tell and pass on stories to the next generation. Active listening is about asking open-ended questions and being curious about the conversation. By asking the questions we learned in journalism school, such as who, what, when, where demonstrates you want to hear more. Some people listen just so they can speak. People enjoy hearing themselves talk. We interrupt others before we finished speaking.

Examples of good questions include: Tell me more about that? What did you think about that? How could you have responded differently? What do you think is the best pathway for us to move forward?

Wait until the other person is finished talking. Seek the clues that someone is now done speaking. Take a moment to pause before we start to share by speaking.

Focus attention on the conversation. Put away your smart phone and limit any other distractions will be much help. When we practice active listening, we are fully engaged in what other people are attempting to say. Joy listens!

Listening is done with sincere love. Our bodies senses the muscles moving at either ends of our mouths and the muscles in our crow's feet, especially as we grow older. Developing a sense of humor should always be present when we speak.

Joy keeps eye contact. This indicates that we are really present and listening. After the other person has spoken, tell them what you heard. This insures that we captured their thoughts and emotions accurately.

You might paraphrase by saying, do my thoughts frustrate you? Or, as many younger people say, "Do you know what I'm saying?" Other things we could share are words about patience, withholding judgment. If the conversation becomes complicated, give time to sort out how each one feels. Understanding when exiting the conversation is best.

Listening is more than paying attention to words. Hearing is easy. Listening is work. Note body language. Hear voice tones. Feel souls. Feel understood. Relate on a soul level. Miscommunication is rampant. When your mind is occupied and you are someplace else, conversations are now impossible. We need to renew the commitment to the art of conversation. Especially in the area of listening to honor the gap between us. We need more than just tweets and emails, texts and posts and to be present with each other. Our humanness cannot continue without conversations. A baby's cries and facial expressions evolve into signs and words that enable people to know our needs. We learn from each other the life-giving rhythm of speaking and listening.

Nonverbal Communication Cues

Communication begins the moment the person to be encountered in conversation walks into your office door. The message begins even before the person says a word.

The person gives us clues with their downward gaze. That non-verbal cue looks awkward and unsure. A low volume "hello" may indicate how they are feeling.

Nonverbal communication cues are not distinct. And so are verbal cues. Both give deep insight. If we are tuned in, e consider the words and how they are spoken. We look at the facial expressions. We observe the eye contact. Gestures and posture form a more complete understanding of the message being shared.

Sometimes facial expressions convey emotions like anger, guilt, anxiety, fear, or joy. Body language communicates more than most people realize. We might be able to sense trust, intimacy, or interest by one's eye contact. Tone of voice signals information including the emotional state, the investment in the shared topic. Physical touch may be a clue about their aggressive approach. A person may grope you tightly or say, "Can I have a hug? Even when they don't know you, they tell you how handsome or pretty you are. Their way of touch might just indicate tat they feel comfortable around you. They might be highly extroverted and touch is their way of expressing affection or respect.

Humor is the shortest distance between a listener and a hearer. Laughter naturally connects us. It is healthy to see the funny side of every event. Being the life and soul of a party indicates that they are connections and a blessing. God is playful.

Smile and stop taking yourself so seriously. Every person on earth smiles in the same language. Smile at everyone. Smile with complete strangers. Smile at children. That is so easy. Smiling uses fewer of our muscles than frowning. Laugh lines are better than frown lines on your face. Pray that the Holy Spirit will give us ears to hear as God hears. And we need to let the words of our mouth honor God. Ephesians 4:29.

God desires one-on-one conversations with each of us. Our Creator has taken the initiative. Plug into the prayerful conversation that has already started. Tell God what is going on in your life. Share your deepest longings. Share your joys. Share your sorrow. Share your fears. Speaking openly strengthens your personal relationship with God.

God loves us more than those close to us, even more than our parents, our spouse, and our dearest friends. God is eager to enable us to show love in relationships. We can all develop and improve as conversationalists. Joy listens!

People do not listen to understand, but to figure out how they will reply. We proclaim, "I just want you to listen." We keep getting distracted by our thoughts. Listening is the conscious decision to understand the words and meanings of the speaker.

Listeners become comfortable with short periods of silence and with pauses. We remain neutral in conversations. Listening does not require an opinion. Choose to simply listen. To have a conversation, we must listen.

Listening is giving someone the opportunity to be heard. We might just see things from the other person's perspective. Faithful listening changes our own hearts and minds. Love never fails.

During the turmoil we are assured by love. We converse with our souls. We listen with our open hearts. Perhaps we connect as we share our coffee.

All people want to be heard. Just because so many of us are quiet, does not mean they have nothing to say. Proverbs 25:11.

Joy listens deeply. When we smile at life, half the smile is for your face. The other half is for somebody else's face.

Joy listens!

Chapter Six

# Joy Hopes!

Living in these difficult times requires us to maintain a hopeful perspective about our future. Mark 13:32-33. World-wide calamity is accelerant. We are experiencing violent disorders. Natural disasters are increasing. Political unrest, economic chaos and wars prevail. Media satisfies an insatiable appetite for witnessing murder, violence, nudity, and sexual impurity.

Most people have resigned themselves to accept the cruelty and wickedness as never to be gone. Most have given up their hope. They have surrendered to despair. Hoping and wishing are differing things. Hope without faith and our faithfulness is empty. Hope is full and active. Wishing does nothing. The power is placed outside of us. Hope causes our feelings to be lighter. We are always moving between our memories and hope. Hebrews 6:19-20.

## Hope as My Wife Fights Cancer

My wife's test was positive for breast cancer. Her condition was critical. We did know exactly how to respond. Despite our feelings, our world changed. A new world rushes in.

Nothing is the same.

Our family and friends shared our concern about the diagnosis and the procedures to undergo. We held on to he hope in God's promises. Romans 8:28.

Our Creator knows our body better than we or the doctors know. God knows our bodies inside and out. We were fearfully and wonderfully made. We did not know how to handle this. Psalm 139. Life was interrupted for both of us.

Some people who are diagnosed with cancer refer to it as the Big C. The Big C in us is Christ. Days, especially after chemotherapy, were uncomfortable. She just could not find comfort emotionally, physically, or spiritually. The medicine did not overpower her. Her doctor had assured her that this was not her fault.

Love from family and friends warmed her like a comforter on a cold night. She refused to lose heart. Zephaniah 3:16-17. In her silent and spoken prayers, she asked for clarity of mind, wisdom, compassion, and joy. She asked for grace to accept everything she and I could not understand.

She kept up her involvement in a Christian congregation. She shared her gift of playing the piano despite her pain. What a joy to be part of the family of Christ. She received enough letters and cards to fill a book. I Corinthians 2:26.

She knows that she is a part in the body of Christ. When the body of Christ works together as one, healing grace flows freely. The many days when she was not feeling well, life was overwhelming. Pain sapped her motivation. It blurred her focus. Isaiah 43:2.

God walked beside us. The Creator provides the help and hope. Deuteronomy 33:25. We have counted on the changeless faithfulness of God whatever comes to mark the life journey. Psalm 23:4. After weeks of travel for chemotherapy sessions, bills at the pharmacy, appointments with many specialists in cancer care, a wig, and just so many hassles that became more than our routines than we could have imagined.

Her days and nights seemed so long. She kept being tired and exhausted. Her genuine prayers bombarded the throne of God's grace and love. She discovered her hope in God alone. Psalm 119:49-50.

She continues to keep going through the emotional and physical turmoil that serious illness causes. Place your hope in what we will experience one day with God. Jesus has promised that Jesus is on the other side of our life journey. United with those who have gone before us in heaven will be a grand bonus.

Hope is born in faith and trust. Hope grows out of faith and gives meaning to everything we do. Hope is a precious principle by which to live. Hope helps faithfulness to develop. If we lose our wealth, we lose nothing. If we lose our health, we lose something. If we lose hope, we lose everything.

Hope in Christ gives us a different way to think. This hope gives us a different life to live. Fueled by our expectations, our lives will build with noting but hope. We can face death with hope. Psalm 33:20-22.

For millions of Christians, hope of Christ is the source of survival of horrible odds under unspeakable circumstances.

Douglas McGurk wrote his dissertation at Queens' University in Belfast, Northern Ireland in 2022. He delves into the sermons of Jean Medard, pastor of the French Reformed Protestant Church in Rouen during war time. These sermons answer the question about "what to say" The German Nazis had traumatized the people of France. These sermons were a brave and constant response to the abnormal circumstances subsumed by war.

This research is being excellent. It shows that pastors regularly and repeatedly guided their congregations in response to God. His work exposes a little-known history of a scripturally based response to oppression through the love of others, and the power of the joy of the Lord. (Douglas McGurk, "An Examination of the Sermons of Pastor Jean Medard in the French City and District of Rouen, 1939-1945," 325 pages)

Medard reminded his congregation of the joy to be experienced and expressed in thee unspeakable times of darkness. (Douglas McGurk, Ibid., p. 244)

In a Christmas sermon in 1941, he said that to close one's eyes against what was happening in the world around them would be a hideous act. There would be no hunkering down waiting for the barrage to pass. (Douglas McGurk, Ibid., p. 245)

Medard's powerful and faithful preaching is illustrated in a note from a Mr. Plard, a member of Medard's congregation, written in April 1942. He told his pastor that his son Henri had been arrested in Paris. He would spend tree months in the Dancy Camp for publicly wearing a yellow star to show Christian solidarity with the Jews.

The summary of the note were these words, "My son has been arrested by the Gestapo and imprisoned in Drancy, and it is because of your preaching and teaching." (Douglas McGurk, Ibid., p. 3)

He told them that with enough courage, then, the faithful would know the joy of salvation, the joy of Christmas, for Christ reveals the image of the invisible God. That is sufficient when things in life are not going well.

Imagine today your living in hope. Imagine your life is going well. Your relationships are easy and smooth. Enjoy hopeful expectations. Really feel the hope that will eliminate your fears. Believe in your possibilities. Hope keeps us in a frame of mind while we are waiting.

Optimistic speaker and writer Dale Carnegie noted, "Most of the important things in the world have been accomplished by people who have kept on trying when there seemed to be no hope."

Think about your most difficult challenge. Reframe and revise how you think about it. Work with your will and use faith and hope in the environment and find a way to love all involved in your situation.

Expect that there will come insight and clarity. Perhaps the right people will come into your life, or a differing situation will emerge. Be watchful. Listen carefully for information and wisdom that is communicated to you.

The war-time devastated congregation in northern France continues to celebrate Christmas with an uncertain future.

The following sermon was preached in Rouen on April 7, 1940. Medard said, "It is a wisdom that we preach, a wisdom not of this age. We preach the wisdom of God." His was delivered one month before the German invasion of France.
The pastor finished his sermon saying, "Our response must be, here I am, even and especially in a time of war." (Douglas McGurk, Ibid., pp. 71-73)

## Patience and Hope

We must wait for God's timing. We want what we want now. Hope includes our work, our persistence, and effort. Being full of hope causes us to be colorful, zestful, and alive. Hope

69

increases our life force through spiritual and physical breath. Every cell in our body is strengthened.

We must stay patient. Hope and faith are needed to keep us alive and to heal us. There are no hopeless situations, only people who are hopeless about them. Hope gives us persistence, willpower, courage, strength and joy that hopes. Hopelessness takes these strengths away.

Every moment exercise your hope and faith that the heavenly world exists. God makes good out of bad things. God brings light into darkness.

Wait patiently, with hopeful expectations. Take the right actions with your soul's hope. Feel gratitude, knowing that there is always hope. It is called the grace of God.

Heaven is on the mind of the most joyful Christians. Even writers of our most famous hymns changed gears in the last verse from the earthly to the heavenly. We sing from "many dangers, toils, and snares" to "when we've been there ten thousand years." Living life with the hope of heaven is the best way to renew joy.

The incessant call to dream concerning our future. We live in the present. In the now, we desire more. The present time does not satisfy our souls. The vision quest for more is at the root of biblical hope.

When we lose hope, we stop telling stories. Hope is the dream of peace, the anticipation of joy as we envision what is not yet. II Corinthians 4:16- 18.

Hope and the Eyes of Faith

Hope sees with eyes of faith which is the wind in the sails tat takes faith forward into the future. Hebrews 11:1. Hope

70

presses on to imagine the total fulfillment that will drench us in joy.

"Our companion, guide, and comfort on the great journey into joy is he Holy Spirit. At the onset, it is the Spirit who inspires joy when grace has opened us to receive God's Word. When' life's perplexities impoverish us, it is the Spirit who, working through the gift of joy, remove all boundaries to our hope." (John Mogahgah, *Alive Now!*)

We enjoy happiness in our circumstances, but it seems not enough. The joy of the Lord will carry us through challenging times. God's gift of joy lifts our hope.

Hopeful Christians open themselves to joy. They cultivate a soul- environment where joy roots and grows. Gazing on Christ is to reflect on Jesus' life, death, and resurrection, and to share time with others. Look for glimpses of Christ in the world.

There is eternal hope for our transformation with the renewing of our minds. Romans 12:2. So express gratitude for every day. Thank God s you cultivate joy and hope. Tell other people how grateful you are for their presence in your life. (Gina Manskar, "Cultivating Joy, *Alive Now!*)

Reframe your life experiences. Hope transforms the times when we limit our perspective of possibilities. Consider whether the difficulty you now experience can become a place to encounter Christ. John 1:5.

Allow uncertainty to exist. Trust in God's grace. Ask Christ to walk with you. Share yourself with others in a spirit of support by offering kind words, encouragement, and hope.

Keep hope alive. Read the Bible for assuring yourself that you are loved. Do not allow your hope to fade.

May the Holy Spirit help us find the joy of knowing God's love and sharing it with others. Here is a close connection between hope and joy. Joy is our thinking and action now. Hope is how we imagine we might act in the future.

Hope must not get in the way of today. Hope is never a prisoner of our memories. Hope still lies in the future. Hope increases as we dream new dreams.

## Hope and New Beginnings

Hope brings us the day of new beginnings. We move on into the future with confidence that God is good. Hope is the soil of our faithfulness which is living for something bigger than ourselves. Encounters that force us to struggle, surrender and wait are required. Hebrews 11:13-16.

We refuse to allow powerlessness to silence or shake off confidence in God. We long to be free of disappointment. We yearn to burst free of constraints of our of the flesh, the world, and our soul. Freedom enables us to admit the powerlessness, our emptiness, and our desire to be loved by God and others.

Hope is not old endings but new beginnings.

## Hope and Joy

Hope is based on "not yet." Hope is a presentiment that our imagination and dreams are more real than present reality. Hope says that the frontiers of the possible are not determined by the limits of what is actual.

Hope involves patience. Self-denial. Postponement of gratification, Discipline. Hope is a future that remains outside our own time living one earth.

Joy is related to hope. Hope involves embracing new relationships and possibilities of action. If hope is loosening the constraints of reality, so we can discern the potential of the reality in our current circumstances. We are always in the midst of beginning again.

Joy is the deep pleasure and emotional energy generate when hope and joy converge. Joy is generated with our feeling of challenge and transcendence coming from overcoming boundaries and barriers, while we encounter new possibilities. Praying to the One who invites us to hope, to slow down, to breathe deeply, to draw near. Without breath in our lungs, we die. Job 33:4, John 20:22, Ezekiel 37:5.

The Bible gives us breath prayers. Numbers 6:25-28, Psalm 18:6, 62:1, 118:14, 119:76, 147:3, I John 4:18, Mark 4:39. Hope comes as we sail turbulent waters with prayer.

Remember, hope waits. Hope does not sit idly, whittling our lives away. Anticipate the joy that is coming. We give God glory by loving others. Evil intends for us to resign to powerlessness and giving up on our future. We can then dance with joy with an unbridled passion.

God's spending time waiting for us is incomprehensible. God refuses to lose hope. Love is knowing God feels love for us. It is for joy that we love. III John 4. The fullness of joy gives an overall view of our past, present, and future from our eternal now.

Love is the spiritual fruit of the memories of faith and the desires of hope. We love because God first loved us. I Corinthians 13:4-7. Love is the most profound risk of our life journey.

73

In our writing and preaching, my mentor John Killinger and I used the French word jouissance. Joy is a strong word, but it is too often separated from our sensuality. Jouissance means knowing joy in the senses of smell, sight, touch, sound, and taste. John Killinger served on the staff and preached in the famed American Church in Paris. All his tastes of joy were sweet.

Everything is now for God, so we can live our earthly journeys with joyous anticipation and clear expectation. Joy is a taste of the presence of God. God surprises us with glorious and graceful love.

We live wholeheartedly and passionately in the present. Our entire lifetime journey is needed to find out how our past shapes the future. Seize the present with insight and vision.

Hope invites us to become the people we were created to be. Hope plunges us into new relationships with new goals and divine purposes. We sit on the porch in silence and wait for God.

Hope frees us from the regrets of our past, and the fears for the future, and the emptiness of now. Our thinking centers on our relationship with the Creator and how we can serve. Serving God is bringing our life story to allow the themes to share the story of God.

To be more human is to be willing to live with an indifference toward our own future plans as we join God and the dreams of others. We are to love those whom God has placed during all the years of our journey.

God has given us our unique stories to make it known how God has worked to transform us. We are being redeemed in a distinct way. God calls each one of us to exist in a particular part of the earth with specific people.

We will be entangled with a story every day. These encounters potentially change lives. We are to live with openness and expectant hope.

We might think of ourselves as well and happy today. During any war, millions will be forced to be surprised that war has come to a nation who now must sacrifice themselves. The power of sharing our joy is clear on what is expected of the faithful.

Ordinary women and men continue to express joy and enthusiasm, to be ready to give, and ready to hold on to their eternal lives. To seek the eternal kingdom of God means not attempting to be detached from the things of earth, so that any consideration that any struggle, pain and suffering is unchristian and beneath one's dignity.
Faithfulness is becoming involved in supporting others. To overcome and endure is possible. Just as we give support for those in war in Ukraine, such as sending parcels to prisoners, as France and others have struggled for freedom.

Joy hopes!

# Chapter Seven

# Joy Serves!

God came into this world in the form of Jesus. He did not come as a king. He was a servant. Philippians 2. The heart of a genuine servant is a joyful one. Joy abounds in the places of service. Psalm 100:2.

Serving God brings joy to your soul. God is the source of ultimate joy. Serving the Lord with gladness is the way to live. Jesus' command to serve and worship God is to be accomplished joyfully.

Joy serves! And we have to invite others to serve. Wholehearted obedience brings joy. Living a life of faith and faithfulness involve our entire person. I Corinthians 15:58. Our service will always bring a good return as we remain in God's service every day of our lives.

Everything we do serves God. Colossians 3:23-24. In the long run, we are not serving other people through our service. We serve to honor God. Our service is called a sacrifice of praise. Romans 12:1. We are open to whatever God has in store for us. We were appointed to serve by Jesus the Christ. I Timothy 1:12. Becoming a Christian and giving your life to Christ allows him to give you the opportunity to serves God's purposes. Jesus will give us strength to do the service. Serve God wherever the Lord has placed us.

## The Joy of Service

The whole world would be filled with joy if we did acts of kindness. Rabindranath Tagore's quote on service and joy hangs on my office wall.

"I slept and dreamt that life was joy. I awoke and saw that life was service. I acted and behold, service was joy."

The word service gives us a daunting feeling for doing a task we do not want to do. A judge may give "community service" to be part of our sentence for doing something wrong. Most high schools require their students to do community service for people who live near the school.

Service is an act of helpful activity. We serve our family and friends by sharing our joy. All people can serve, regardless of the age. I helped my mother with setting the table or helping wash dishes. I mowed my grandmother's lawn with a push mower beginning when I was about nine years old. Service is always helpful.

When we serve, we exercise our better selves. Service becomes a way of life. Every act of service has a spiritual quality. We acknowledge by our acts of service that we are sisters and brothers to each other. We share a common home during our earthly journey.

That quality within us is expressed as joy. Service is an expression of love. We rarely hear a thank you after we serve. Our church has established a wonderful food bank that serves the homeless. Many families depend on their box of food in order to live.

Without an exception, every person who gave their service at the food bank said they felt "great," after completing their service. That "great" joy response is a "thank you" that we give ourselves.

Jesus is the only way to restore our relationship with God. Jesus is trusted for our salvation and for the service we are called to do. Jesus preached that we serve others and seek their good over our own. Find ways to serve others and make less of ourselves.

Life is a place of service. We don't serve someone else when we are born and helpless. Perhaps our only service is to enable our parents to feel proud and happy.

At the other end of life when we are dying or on our deathbed, we cannot physically serve. In the years of between time, we serve and are served constantly. Our lifetime on earth is hard to bear at times, but in our faithfulness, life ends with eternal joy.

Being blessed and overflowing with the goodness of God in our lives causes us to feel the joy of the Lord. Remember your personal salvation journey. Remember when you desired to do just anything in church. Recall your excitement and love for God as you were empowered to "do something for Jesus." Nothing was better than serving God. Things happen. We were given menial jobs. Some leaders may have disappointed you. A spouse or your children turned their backs on the Lord.

Regardless of what happened, we all get to the point when we lose the joy of our service. Situations arise that discourage us or cause us to just want to give up.

A Fresh Way to Look at Service

Janet Ruth Gendler has written about Service in a fresh way. She wrote, "Service is devotion's practical sister. She is a funny one, sort of austere and sensuous at the same time. She isn't as stern as she used to be when she was a child. Service has learned that seeds must be watered before they sprout. Some lie dormant for years. Shoots must be nourished before they bloom. We all work in service in different ways.

"Sometimes we have to remind Service to take a vacation. She sees so   much that needs to be done. She forgets that she also needs to rest. Service could be a tremendous job counselor. She never asks to do what you cannot do, but only what you mostly can do." (Janet Ruth Gendler, *The Book of Qualities*, pp. 82-83)

We all face these feelings. We feel like we are at the end of our rope. The motions continue, but the joy is gone. We keep on keeping on.

Some people criticize me as being obsessed by my service with joy. Taylor Swift sings about people throwing stones at those who shine. My publisher says that I am the definition of prolific. Others have said that I am "a preaching machine." God has given me endless energy.

Focus on serving the Lord. Psalm 100. Don't focus on serving your pastor. Don't even focus on the church. People lose joy when they are not serving God, but perhaps only to be seen by others.

Serving God keeps our hearts tender. Regardless of the tasks or the compensation we receive. Living a life of joyful service is a privilege as we demonstrate our love for Christ.

Keep Christ in the forefront of all service we do. Delighting in serving God brings us contentment. Any response of others is in the Holy Spirit by the grace of God. I Thessalonians 1:4-5.

Human beings exalt themselves with their pride. Needing the grace of God, we do nothing without the power of God. Response to our service is not because of any merit, but because of the special love of God.

Even though it is God's Spirit that empowers us to joyfully serve, God can use things and other people to bring us back to divine enjoyment. I Thessalonians 2:13.

## The Effect of Joyful Service

When the Holy Spirit works in us, it brings delightful effects. The radical Good News is rooted in joy. The joy of the Lord is our strength that fills our hearts in any situation. The Gospel enables us to live in joy, to interpret our services in a way that is eternal.

Christ's resurrection powerfully demonstrates that any suffering is temporary, but God's love and power are forever. The effect of joyful service serves the interests of God in this earthly journey. We serve God in the everyday events of life. I Thessalonians 1:3.

We are called to serve God and others. Those who serve have lower rates of mental illness and criminal acts. Christians connect with the underground stream of joy by constantly communicating about our awareness of God being present.

When I was ordained to do ministry, I resolved that I would never turn anybody away. I have tried to be faithful to my promise, but it wasn't easy. Even Paul felt the difficulty. Romans 7:15. Burning within me is the flame of God's love and grace. I admit tat I have encountered sick humans who tend to manipulate, and I did always indulge them.

Many of my encounters started with annoyance and difficulty. Most ended with joy. Giving people my time is my gift in service. My willingness to give my time in later life was natural for me. Jesus told Pete to "feed my lambs." John 21:17. These words still have a powerful influence on me.
People now living throughout the world left their previous way of serving. The effect of joyful service is seen in every hamlet

and abode of the world. Joy serves! What a power joy is.

I can't say how God has done miracles as I have used the printed word, radio, television that has reached out to millions. I spent money and much time earning degrees in journalism at the University of Missouri in Columbia and numerous seminaries.

Being willing to attend the best schools in the world. I honed my talents and skills as I was asked to serve in public relations to promote the 22 programs of the Sunday School Board of the Southern Baptist Convention.

I experienced so much joy from emails and letters from people who benefited from something I spoke or wrote.

Going back to a church where I served, countless people told me that they became Christians when I encountered them with my service that became a joy for me. I spoke at the 100th homecoming anniversary at Woodlawn Baptist Church in Bristol, Tennessee. What joy I felt when people told me what my service to the Lord meant to them.

Of course, I have had my own share of hardship, but this is nothing compared to the joy of serving the Lord. The joy and privilege of serving as a minister, an ambassador for Christ. Today, I have no regrets.

Perhaps one of our joys in heaven will be for those saved by love and grace to tell you that they are there in eternal joy because of some service that I did during my earthly journey. Joy serves! Joy brings us closer to the glory of God. Dreaming the dreams of God makes me fully alive. Even before we accomplish anything, the process of dreaming about doing good brings our callings to life. Our dreams and desires form character and create our destinies.

I have often prayed and focus on the prayer attributed to Francis of Assisi. It has been quoted in many articles and books and in pulpits throughout the world.

"Make me an instrument of Thy peace. Where there is hatred, let me sow love, where there is injury, pardon, where there is doubt, faith, where there is despair, hope, where there is darkness light, and where there is sadness, joy.

Divine Master, grant that I may not seek to be consoled, as to console, to be understood, as to understand, to be loved, as to love.

For it is in giving that we receive, it is in pardoning that we are pardoned, and it is in dying that we are born to eternal life."

## Life Is the Place of Service

Leo Tolstoy wrote, "Life is a place of service, and in that service one has to suffer a great deal that is hard to bear, but most often to experience a great deal of joy. However, that joy can be real only if people look upon their life as a service and have a definite object in life outside themselves and their personal happiness."

Joy serves!

# Chapter Eight

# Joy Reads!

Nothing brings joy like a well-written book. During the long Nebraska winters, I enjoy getting cozy and comfortable as I read a good book. Embracing the joy of reading, I fully appreciate all the good it brings into my life. My brothers and I spent countless hours in the Bristol Public Library, checking out books and toting them home. Our joy of reading expose s to the vast world of information and endless imagination available between the covers of a book.

Our communities are vital for listening for the direction of the Holy Spirit. Romans 12:1-2, Mark 3:34-35. The need for community in our earthly journey has led to the creation of churches which are at the root of preparation for everlasting joy.

Joy reads! The access to books is unprecedented. Books are everywhere. We may buy a book for forty bucks, but no one else will buy it, even for a few bucks. People don't know how to evaluate a good book. We read books on the phone, tablets, computers, or listen to them read in our cars. We can order books online. We can purchase them in a store. We have access to many public and college libraries.

Reading is crucial but reading books for our spiritual growth in not about the number of books or pages read. It is about remembering and using what we have read. The joy of reading connects us with God through the writers. One benefit is discovering deep moments of insight, renewal, and affirmation.

Reading is an essential path for understanding God through both contemporary and ancient writers. A book written to spiritually guide its readers has a set of qualities. Book reading for myself has drawn me into the presence of God. Book demonstrate classic discipline to contemporary life. I begin to love God out of desire, not duty.

The recent invention of computers has not done away with reading. In the early church wrote carefully and painstakingly words on parchment. What if when the printing press was invented, and Christian leaders said that they saw no use to reading? Those who did not learn to read would have accomplish nothing for 500 years.

If it were not for the printing press, the Reformation may not have happened. Martin Luther's use of printed material including the Bible translated into the German language would have never been such a powerful instrument.
We reflect on writings going back to the early church fathers. Their literary works include a biblical perspective with appreciation for how scripture comes alive.

We can read books from other nations of the world. We can have books shipped from seven continents. Reading is good for our spiritual, physical, and mental health. Reading reduces stress, increases intelligence, expands understanding, and improves memory. Reading is to the mind what exercise is to the body.

Opening a book is a positive distraction that has the power to bring unlimited goodness to our lives. As an introvert, I enjoy my quiet time alone. Most people are extraverts. They prefer social activities and networking that connects them to many people. Reading can be social. My wife has a women's book club. There are innumerable discussion groups. I have enjoyed reading to my daughter and grandson and children in my church.

Reading should not be presented to our children as a chore or duty, but as a precious gift. High and endurable is the blessing and the privilege of reading a book. Embrace the joy of reading. Go back and read one of your favorite books. Reading it anew can ignite and give you a reminder of your joy of reading.

The purpose of reading is not just obtaining knowledge. It is part of the human experience. Life is better. We come to understand ourselves. Books are friends we can count on. Drinking a cup of green tea and reading first thing in the morning has become my sanctuary. This routine has provided me a more well-rounded view of the world.

Books are pieces of wisdom passed down from writers who have been there and done that. Books have the power to change our perspective. As a guide to living our own lives, books spark our inspiration and imagination.

Reading the Bible is an incredible source of joy. We enjoy using commentaries and study resources. Joy surrounds us as we sit back, relax, and read the Word of God. The Bible is a fountain every Christian should drink from frequently.

The psalmists tapped into the source of joy often. Psalm 19:8, 119:14, 162. Joy results from having the Word of God dwell in me. Joy is not only something felt within, but joy is cultivated. Reading Scripture cultivates and leads us to live in joy. Reading the Word of God completes our joy. John 15:11.

Reading gives us assurance during times of difficulty and daily testing. Acts 5:41, Romans 5:3, James 1:2, I Peter 4:12-13.

Writers are readers. People ask me, "When did you know you were going to be a writer?" There are many answers. Becoming a writer is a way of moving through the world. Writing is a way of seeing, hearing, and believing.

When I think about how my books came to be, I think of all the other books that have come and are yet to come. I have learned more about the world with my reading and writing has given me something to believe in, a better self-esteem, and joy.

## The Habit of Reading

The joy of reading continues as we become older. We carve out time for reading. Reading is a most important habit. My prayer is that my books will pass on a bit of my experience.

Reading alters the neural pathways in our brains. It allows us to make new connections across different disciplines. Reading contributes to salvation. The process of eternal salvation comes through the opportunity to learn from a diversity of voices that make up the kingdom of God. John 3:16 is he mission statement for te church on earth and God's eternal kingdom of joy.

Rereading is something I am doing all the time. When I re-read the Bible, I find something different every time. What joy there is when a new interpretation challenges me to understand better. Joy reads.

So my readers embarking on their journey of life are fully alive. To enjoy your journey, start living. The rest of life is before you. Go write your first page. Realize you can and will revise it.

At times, I tend to overwrite in my articles and books. Getting too abstracted to make sense, I read authors who are authentic and unfussy. Reading enables my writing ministry. Without endurance, perseverance, inspiration, and the grace of God equip me, or I would certainly fall on my face. Actually, I have fallen many times. Technology trips me. The font and design of this book requires hours of work. One word. One article. One book at a time.

The joy of reading lets joy sink into our souls. Reading hammers home the essential points of faith, trust, will, and calling to serve. My writing is more polished and poised these days. Writing is both art and practice.

Some of the stories we read enhances our spirit and leads us to that eternal joy which is often the subject of what we read and learn. It has brought joy to millions to turn off the television and read. We have become couch potatoes as many are glued to the TV. Half the time spent in front of a TV set is time watching commercials.

Daily news can be toxic. Too much exposure to the ways and woes of the world limits the possibilities for your joy. With God's help, we can turn our lives around as we use the gift of reading to make us whole.

## Reading the Writing of Others

When our thoughts come against a blank wall, we can turn to read the writings of others, who have expressed their inner lives. Parts of each day for significant reading that directs us to everlasting joy. We can even have conversations with the dead through reading. Reading history and the biographical stories of people who lived in the past eons and human ages, gives us knowledge unheard of in he past. The history of language and why there are more and more nations being established. People can never forget their culture and the pain of living under the power of a dominating empire. New countries such as South Sudan, the Balkans, and the former Union of Soviet Socialist Republics have been established.

Before the invention of all the new technology we gained knowledge through reading. Reading improves our focus and concentration. Read every day for your entire life and you will become a better writer. Your analytical skills will enable problem solving. Your vocabulary will expand. Knowledge gives us more power to know. Knowledge is something nothing or no one can take away from you.

We direct and evaluate our reading according to our needs during any particular time. Meeting together in the presence of members of a book club is effective. We might have to create our own group. Perhaps your group will evolve into a sharing group. Group members experience similar difficulties. Sharing our inward struggles keeps us on track for avoiding our problems indefinitely.

Reading as a spiritual practice helps us grow closer to God. Books are wonderful resources to connect us with wise teachers who lived centuries ago. We become transformed into the image of God. II Corinthians 2:3:16-18. Reading is a major part of our spiritual formation and our uncovering God's call to us. Reading becomes the curriculum for Christlikeness.

Computers are said by many is important as the invention of writing. My now 20-year-old grandson could read and use a computer. At age two, he climbed up on a stool and typed Kids.com. When John von Neumann invented the modern computer, he said," I don't really know how useful this thing will be."

Fifty years from now, our great grandchildren will look at our old computers and we can hear them say, "Isn't that funny, they thought computers should look like typewriters."

Never get too busy to read. Do not enter into the thinking of those who simply do not care to read. Joy reads!

Some college graduates never read another book following graduation. So sad for them. We can bring a person to the water, but we can't make her drink.

# Chapter Nine

# Joy Celebrates!

In joy, I feel jubilation. Joy floods in as I look into her eyes, and I say, "I do." Joy finds me skipping rocks on the lake, two brothers by my side. I smile at Ethan at age five, leaping, grabbing the monkey bar, swinging, flying, running. Our family enjoys fireworks on the fourth of July. Romping through the lawn with my dog Brownie, playing chase. Sitting in front of the fireplace, slipping warm drinks. I sit above a high Appalachian Mountain top deep in the Great Smokies with my grin spreading. Walking on stage, turning toward the graduation audience, beaming as the doctoral hood is draped over my shoulders. That's how I celebrate joy.

Joy flows from inside out. Joy bubbles up and erupts in our soul. Joy is an intense celebrative positive feeling that results in a smile, a laugh, or jumping up and down in delight. Celebrations in Israel involved music. I know we do not celebrate enough. Of all people, we have so much to celebrate.

Shallow things pass for celebration. Unbridled celebrations marked significant events. Psalm 81 is what my Hebrew professor called "a festive song." It was written for celebrating the new year. Asaph, the composer, wrote it for the Feast of Tabernacles.

New seasons remind us of where we have been. They celebrate the anticipation of what lies in the immediate future.

Celebrating joy in ordinary moments, gratitude and joy are one. Every joy speaks to those who listen. Life is brief. Working with the elderly reminds me of life's brevity.

Caress the celebration of what you have. Release what is no longer yours. Trust God for your future joy. Psalm 150:6. Join the celebration chorus of creation. Allow the joy of God to breathe in your weary soul.

Faithful love infuses life's ordinary with joy. God steps into every moment of our days. Psalm 16:11. Definitions for celebration are performing ceremony publicly with appropriate rites, marking an anniversary by festivities, observing a holiday, observing a notable occasion.

I celebrated 70 years of ministry in 2023. The celebration was something I never anticipated could be a reality. We have all enjoyed recognition ceremonies at our work, at annual conference meetings, and regional assemblies. In the Holston Conference my churches received 20 gold medals and a silver for excellence in evangelism. Celebrate your church's anniversaries. That is a wonderful way to celebrate with some fun, recognition, and unity.

## Wisdom from Experience

Achieving longevity in my walk with God is so beautiful. Dramatic late- life conversions are wonderful. Psalm 71:5.

We owe so much to those who have gone before us. I have been blessed with several mentors in my personal, academic, and professional life. It is pure joy as we recognize and acknowledge the wisdom and experience of people who are older than we are.

As I review my years of ministry, I meditate with Psalm 71 which reflects what seasoned seeks can proclaim through their experience. They have confidence in God. Psalm 71:5. God is heir refuge of strength. Psalm 71:7.

They depend on God's salvation and righteousness. Psalm 7:15. They have known personally God's mercy and miracles. Psalm 71:17. They appreciate God's faithfulness. Psalm 71:22. Wisdom flourishes and bears fruit in old age. Psalm 92:12, 14.

The Christian Church (Disciples of Christ) honored my service as moderator of the Nebraska Region with a lovely plague. I continued to play the tapes when the regional minister handed me the honor during a board meeting.
Any time is a good time for a joyful celebration. Celebrate big and small things. Celebrate all your milestones. Team celebrations bring positive outcomes. Celebrations improve productivity by recognition. Joy celebrates and reenforces victories. It's an opportunity to celebrate accomplishments during these challenging times.

Psalm 86 gives us an outline for us to put things and God, in proper perception. David writes of Gods provision. Psalm 86:1-7. He refers to God's position in Psalm 86:8-10. God's power for our empowerment is sung with joy. Psalm 86:11-16.

Celebration helps us feel comfortable and confident. Feeling appreciated does tons for self-esteem, uplifting our moods and performance. Appreciation is fundamental for retaining those with talents and gifts. Never hesitate to celebrate our God who is loving, graceful, and the Creator of all that is.

Living a Life of Celebration

The best biblical source about living a life of celebration is the Old Testament book of Nehemiah. At the dedication celebration of the completion of the wall of Jerusalem, Levites were there to celebrate joyfully with songs of thanksgiving. Music was shared on harps, lyres, and cymbals. Nehemiah 12 and 13:1-3.

It is vitally important to practice the celebrations. One spiritual life uses celebration as a essential part. We see celebrations throughout the Word of God. The wise men, the shepherds, and angels celebrated the birth of Jesus with gifts, songs, and prayer.

Scripture makes it plain and clear that celebration is a discipline that God wants us to practice. God desires Christians to celebrate. The Bible tells us that Christ came so that we have life and life more abundantly. John 10:10. The people of Israel had a great celebration when dedicating the wall. The story gives principles about how joy celebrates. The Word of God says the Israelites established a special time for celebrating he Lord's faithfulness by dedicating the wall to God. They carefully planned.

We celebrate on Sundays in the church. Other celebrations bring joy on a personal level with the believing community. God's faithfulness can be celebrated in numerous ways. None of these festivities go without deliberate planning.

We practice celebration by dedicating everything to God. Nehemiah 12:43, 47. The people responded to their leaders by gathering to read the Word of God and giving daily portions for the singers and the keepers of the gate. The joy of the leaders had an effect on many others. The rest of the entire Bible teaches that our joy as leaders, affects others. Proverbs 17:22.

The primary purpose of the celebration in Nehemiah was to dedicate the wall to God. Dedications are special ceremonies which picture what e practice every day. We do these things to glorify God. I Corinthians 10:31. We find ways to dedicate everything to God. Living without dedication is life without the joy of celebration.

We offer our bodies, our time, our relationships, and our projects to God with prayer. We thank God for everything. We dedication our best work to God. Joy celebrates out of a right relationship with God. Philippians 4:4, Psalm 1:1.

Joy celebrates the promises of God. Nehemiah 12:37-39. The people walked around the wall in different directions. God asked Abraham to lift his eyes and survey the land and to walk through it. Genesis 13: 14-17.

Joshua was called to walk around Jericho seven times to symbolize God's giving them that city before the walls of Jericho tumbled down. They conquered the city. Joshua 6.

Claiming the promises of God is a necessary requirement for living with the joy of celebration. Christians live without joy celebrations because they take God's promises for granted. There are more than 3,000 promises in the Bible. We have to claim them by our faith and our faithfulness.

Many Christians are walking around without the power of joy because they neglect thanking God. They pour water on the Spirit's fire. This affects both themselves and their community. Living with the joys of celebration, we must put logs on the fire of God. We do this by confessing our sins. Nehemiah 12:30-31.

Before the dedication started, the Levites purified themselves. Similarly, we cannot know the joy of celebration without the continual cleansing of or sin. Psalm 32:2-5.

God wants our best. We must make sincere investments. Malachi 1:6-9. People give God the scraps of their time and service. Proverbs 11:25. God promises to give us a life filled with tremendous joy as we give our lives. God will give the ability to live a life of celebration, a life flourishing with joy.

Part of joyful celebration was being devoted to scripture. That is true for us as well, Honor the Word of God and obey it. The Word revives the soul and brings joy to the heart.

Dear readers, live a life of joyful celebration by dedicating everything to God, planning times of celebration, leading with joy, giving thanks in everything, continually confessing our sins, claiming the promises of God, investing in the house of God, and by being devoted to the Word of God.

Joy celebrates!

# Chapter 10

# Joy Plays!

Play imaginative, fun, non-compulsory activity filled with humor and spontaneous lightness. Play and fun go hand in hand. Play totally absorbs the player. Play is not frivolous. The pure playfulness of play is not lost. The value of play is elusive. If we dwell on the pragmatics in play, it ceases to be play.

Play includes imagination. It is creative and spontaneous. Playing is entering a world of make-believe. Play gives needed perception and rest. Living carefully and wisely is to make the most of our brief time on earth. Romans 13:11-13, Psalm 32:6. Play should have trivializing effect on living. If play serves merely to divert rather than to give a faithful perspective, it may prevent serious transformation with the world so badly needing redemption.

God knows the beginning from the end. An eternal perspective calls for diligent engagement with sharing the Good News. It also calls for those who work for God times for needed rest. The grace of God gives freedom to play even during times of suffering in this fallen world. Play and playfulness remind us that there is rest and restoration for the faithful.

## Sabbath Keeping and Restoring Rest

The sabbath allows people to disengage from working for themselves, and to remember the source of heir daily bread. Rest and restoration put their efforts of survival in proper perspective. The people of God rest in the sufficiency of God.

Isaiah rebuked Israel as he seeks to free them from thinking their efforts were the ultimate source for their protection. Isaiah 41:13-14. James corrects a heightened view of human planning. James 4:13-17.

Sabbath keeping is not intended to undercut human effort, diligence, passion, and attentiveness. Human activity is subservient to he plan and power of God. Sabbath rest leads to a childlike trust, dependence, and play with God.

Playfulness is not just for children. Joy plays with intention to integrate more play into our lives. Reclaim your playful self. The results will be a sheer delight. God will make all things new. Revelation 21:5.

Have you ever thought of God as your playmate? The Spirit urges us to play. The serious work of salvation sets the stage for unbridled joy of knowing and loving God. Joy is expressed in playful exuberance. The sense of play has its origin in God.

The Bible tells us about playing of instruments. Music is a playful expression. The biblical words for play mean amusement, celebration, laughter, delight, dancing, leaping, frolicking, and prancing.

## Playful God

There is amazing order in the universe. Nothing happens apart from the Creator's plan. That holy plan culminates in God's glory and our good. God works with playful extravagance.

Lavish divine activity including singing birds, the finest wine, gushing springs and waterfalls, and watered trees are in fabulous display.

The psalmist describes the immense and powerful sea, huge sea creatures. Psalm 104:26. Besides God been the intelligent designer, God is the playful artist. Look at the sheer varieties of sounds, tastes, colors, shapes, and textures.

God is both skillful architect and creative artist. God does nothing based on need. Acts 17:24-25, Psalm 50:9-12. God's pleasure and glory are the primary motives. Matthew 10:26, Luke 11:21, Ephesians 1:5, Isaiah 43:7.

Creation is a source of pleasure and delight in the work of the hands of God. The most moving images of play in scripture occur in the attempts to express the joy experienced in the coming kingdom of God. Zachariah 8:5.

Fearless child-like play, no longer inhibited by the effects of sin is a meaningful metaphor for the kingdom. Isaiah 11:8-9. Similar images of playful celebration and merrymaking abound. Jeremiah 30:18-19, 32:4,13-14. Faith and faithfulness to God invariably leading to childlike play as all creation sees God's fulfilled promises.

Spontaneous, playfulness was sparked by God's presence and blessing displayed by David. The ark of the covenant had been returned from the Philistines. David appears childlike in his dancing and celebrating. II Samuel 6:5, 14, 20-22.

David's playful dancing and leaping mirrors other responses of joy over God's restoring power and presence. Psalm 87:17, 114:4, Isaiah 35:6, Malachi 4:2, Jeremiah 31:4, 13, Luke 1:44, 6:23, Acts 3:8.

Before Jesus called the little children to his side, he must have enjoyed seeing them at play. He knew that play was not only for children. We do not laugh enough. We do not play enough. Joy plays!

Play is defined as doing something you don't have to do. You do it just for the fun. We need to daydream as well as dreaming at other times, including the dreams from our time of sleep. We will find surprising joy if we permit that little child inside us to come out and play. Let go of the world and its cares.

Visualize what you learned to do as a child. Take yourself back in time to when you played as a kid. You were in that moment doing something you loved. Watch the experiences as a movie in your mind. Re-experience the joyful time as if they were happening now. Imagination and make-believe were part of it.

Remember climbing at the playground. It does my soul good to see the children playing at the Elmwood Park that I see clearly from my home office window. Feel again the excitement, the combined calm with mobilized energy, lightheartedness and the sensation of joy.

God has unexpected surprises, discoveries, and joys ahead of us if we let God lead us. Failing to understand the grace of God, we mis out on risking religious decorum. A women in Luke 7:36-50 kissed Jesus feet and used her tears and hair to anoint Jesus' feet with oil. She understood grace.

Another woman "wasted" expensive ointment to anoint Jesus with unrestrained appreciation. Mark 14:3-9.

Flavors of Play

Play comes in many flavors. Listen to the inner signals to find what gives you a playful spirit. Keep visualizing what you loved as a child. You may have enjoyed creating or inventing things. If you enjoyed playing with others as a child, what brings you more connection with others in fun ways. Exploring and learning new things are ignited by adventures like exploring in a nearby park.

Introduce play into your life routines. We often do the same things in the same ways. Jam out to your favorite music. Dancing around the kitchen with a beloved one. Walking in the rain. Splashing in puddles at our feet. Play isn't just for children. Joy plays in the lives of adults as it is for youngsters. Play is the act of engaging in amusement, diversion, or recreation for its own sake. Play is essential to well-being. Play is enormously important. The power of play brings lightheartedness and fun into our earthly journey.

Play stimulates our creativity. Play fosters intimacy. Play increases relaxation. Playing is fun and it reduces stress.

Let Go of Perfection.

Perfection limits our playfulness. Play sweeps us up in a moment. Embrace absurdity. Laugh at your imperfect self. There is absolutely no way to do wrong when you're at play. Having fun is a feeing, not a specific activity. Anything that connects playfulness and flow qualifies as fun. Understand that what's fun for you may not be fun for everyone.

Reflect on memories of things that were particularly fun. Fun does not have to be a mind-bowing experience or an exotic trip. Authentic play gives opportunity for fun. Not everything that claims to be fun is actually fun. Fun comes from tiny and unexpected moments.

Pay attention to small delights. Observe a hummingbird dipping into a flower. See a child dressed up in a dinosaur costume for no reason. Joy feels connected and playful in the moment.

Joy Plays in the Lives of Adults.

Adults benefit from playing as much as children. It sharpens your sense of humor. Whatever style of fun works for you. Know that making time for fun has unbelievable benefits. Play reduces our well-being. Playful adults have more fun, cope with everything better.

Adults who play more experience an active way of living. Make your physical activity fun. Fun causes adults to be more likely to physically move.

Your moods will respond in feelings of joy as we play. Playing with my daughter and my grandson brought excitement and smiles. We enjoyed most everything we played from Candyland to chess.

I have played a lot of things for the first time. Hiking in the Holston Mountains or playing in a creek with friends were the ways I enjoyed each new thing. Each time I do something new, I have a different positive feeling. I enjoy the joy of being surprised.

## First Time Experiences Matter

Some life experiences bring out our emotions. I know I do not clearly recall the long-ago moments. Reaction to the sky on a plane flight was interesting. We rarely try new things. Wired to be wary is the case with many of us. Playing new games expands our comfort zone. There is always a new challenge.

In my time as an old man and a grandpa, the number of new things to do is reduced. Children, youth, and adults need to challenge themselves to get out of comfort zones. Our family continues to do board games, crossword and jigsaw puzzles.

I ask my clients in psychotherapy sessions to imagine playing with joy. They picture themselves in a situation with people they really like and enjoy being with in an activity that is fun. By actually imagining joy feelings or recalling joyful experiences, I have been able to encourage changes. They go on to creating and experiencing more real-life joy.

Memorize playing joy in your body. When you experience a moment of joy in walking, listening to music, being kind, or feeling thankful, don't postpone it or completely miss it. Pause to notice the feelings in your body. Feel the warmth in your chest. Intensify that sensation. Joyologists call this "memorizing" feelings. This helps you reactivate the feelings whenever you wish.

Reframe Your Life in a Positive Way

Expressing and experiencing positive appreciation is beneficial. Some pastors view preaching as a obligation or burden. Stop saying "I have to" to "I get to." This will bring a miraculous and differing perspective.

Experience the bliss of blamelessness. I tell people in my sermons and conversations, "Nobody is to blame. Everybody is responsible." When we self-condemn, resent, or feel guilty, feeling joy is limited. When people get sick, suffer from cancer, doctors say, "It's not your fault."

Everybody makes mistakes. We need to let go of blame. After the painful situation is over, continuing resentment and blame consumes energy. If you have moved away from your ordeal, break the useless habit of self- recriminating. Focus on how you want to feel right now.

Let go of just being busy. Acting busy or actually doing too many things is an anxiety feeling. Take breaks. When I write my books, I take the moments between my work and obligations to pause, close my eyes, breathe deeply, drink a glass of water and feel what it's like to live outside of time.

Reframing our lives, we can think the best of the person involved in a former relationship. Seeing the goodness in someone brings aliveness and reality about that person you may have once admired and adored. Keep looking for positive qualities. Everyone wants to feel safe, accepted, and loved. Notice the positive effect this has on your state of mind. Enjoy it.

There are many things in our relationships that bring joy. Knowing that we have people who loves and cares for us unconditionally is a source of joy.
Being able to share our life journeys with someone who brings out joy, is extremely rewarding. Joy relates. Joy laughs. Joy matters.

There are scores of types of relationships that people experience. In each one, there is the potential for joy to be present. The connection that is created between two people bring he joy of relationship. The connection can be physical, emotional, or spiritual. Connecting on a deep level brings joy.

Joy relates! It is a freely chosen relationship. There need to be no pretense or façade. Joy comes within the relationship. There are plenty of ways to bring joy into a relationship.

Acts of service help. Making breakfast in bed, walking the dog, taking out the trash are simple ways joy relates.

Effective communication brings answers and strengthens the bond. The power of touch including warm hugs, gentile caresses is crucial for keeping the spark alive. Relationships to God, family, friends, and others, including strangers ignites our joy.

This joy reflects the wisdom, peace, and maturity as we walk in conscious companionship in our relationships.

Why Relationships Give Joy

There are many reasons why relationships give us so much joy. One reason is that joy of companionship comes with sharing the life journey. We feel less lonely. Joy relates in supporting us in difficult times. Simply having someone around bring enjoyment and adventure. Joy relates with respect, trust, and communication.

I could expand on each of these parts that joy relates as we anticipate the power to spark joy. By creating excitement and joy in anticipation of a shared experience amplifies the experience.

We might find opportunities just to act silly. If laughter is the pinnacle of joy, silliness is the surest route there. Play at everything. Be comfortable being yourself.

## Focus on Finding Joy

Find joy is your everyday life whenever you have chosen to live. Slow down and be mindful in order to notice and appreciate the joyful little delights as they occur. Add joy to make every day feel wonderful. Good days. Tough days. Ordinary days. Mundane and nothing special days.

If you still want to change your life and your outlook, sprinkle more small delights throughout the day. Thee moment might appear to be insignificant; they make us find much joy where we are and with whoever we live with and serve.

Remember joy is a choice. Remember how you may have acted and finally be safer and less risky with the choice you have made. Nobody is going to make my life magically feel more joyful for me.

We have more control over the ways our days feel than we realize. You have been given the power to make a choice.

Notice the joy that is already there where you can create a space for joy. Clear the clutter. Clean up the mess. Joy never comes easy when your space, your time, and your energy have no breathing room for joy. Be present and mindful enough to notice and appreciate what you have.

Make joy happen. Find the power of play in finding joy. Joy plays! It gives us hope in little breezes that flow into our lives, in the little sights and sounds of people playing, in the flickering sunlight, in the little bursts of laughter, in the twinkle of an eye, or in the smiles while we are playing.

## Hopeful Play

Play is not a distraction or obsession. God's empowerment brings a wonderful conclusion to our suffering in life. Romans 8:28. This assurance is important in a definition of play. Play prepares us to deal with uncertainties of the journey. For those who live in Christ, they have faith in how the world ends, brings a deep enjoyment of play. Play dramatizes a life that ends well. As Mary Tyler Moore said in her television shows, "You are going to make it after all."

The gospel leads us to play. Play expresses the ability to transcend the brokenness of this world. The world is being redeemed. Without hopeful play, we use play to divert from life's problems rather than a hopeful expression. When play becomes simply an end in itself, it is a frivolous idol that keeps humankind from dealing with the human predicament. When play is hopeful, it is grounded in the gospel.

In the play of joy, in the joy of play, I find infinite possibilities. Play sounds like nothing else. Spontaneous. Unselfconscious. Raucous laughter. Unabashed.

I have felt delight in the uninhibited presence of children. A part of my persona tells me all lines in life intersect at a point, regardless of my personal desires.

Hope and despair. Joy and sorrow. Writing and life. Life and writing. Writing life. Living the writing life. These connect together in a splash or in a soft note. Joy deserves cultivation. God's quiet voice tells me that I will reap whatever I sow. Sowing a few more seeds of joy in my living will enable me to feel and enjoy more frequently.

I will continue writing and sharing joy and joying my writing. Playing my little joy notes for as long as I can. We must continue to be childlike. Nothing oozes out joy more than a pillow fight or a tickle session.
Build up a reservoir of joy. We cannot fully love someone until we love ourselves. We can't find joy with another person if we can't find joy for ourselves.

Despite the benefits of sustained love, it's not easy to keep it up. Natural joy in the beginning of a relationship is mostly rooted in the novelty of the situation. What was the first thing that attracted you to each other?

Identifying what we want in a new or future relationship and acknowledge the process in the past times will help us move forward. We cannot help when we fall in love. That's the reality, like it or not.

Loving somebody who doesn't love you brings disappointment. Love is a complicated experience. It's simply impossible to simply turn off our feelings.

Feelings and Facts

Feelings are feelings. Facts are facts. Ask the Holy Spirit to help you in being discerning regarding your feelings. If we equate the presence of God with an experience, or on my feelings, are we to assume we are not now close to Jesus?

Everyone feels all the feelings of anger, guilt, anxiety, fear, and joy. God's word tells us that love conquers fear. Assurance of God's love does not depend on our feelings. Salvation is the finished work of Christ Jesus. We are in God's presence through faith. Ephesians 2:6.

Scripture tells us "love is of God." I John 4:18. Everything God does is with love. The emotion fear is the fear of the judgment of God. Those who are in Christ know the love of God. This love drives away the fear of condemnation. Romans 8:1. Nothing can separate the faithful believer from the love of God in Christ. Romans 8:38-39, John 3:17.

The unconditional love of God never will not wax and wane. Love is not fickle. It is more than just an emotional feeling. Divine love takes away our fear. Luke 12:32.

The spirit of timidity and fearfulness does not come from God. I John 4:18. Overcoming fear requires total trust in God. Trusting God is refusing to give in to fear. Psalm 5:11. The word perfect in I John 4:18 is best translated as "complete" or "mature."

Fear of punishment is driven out by God's perfect love. I Thessalonians 5:9, I Corinthians 11:13. All human emotions are needed for fear of the Lord is the beginning of wisdom.

## Heaven as Eternal Play

The saving power of God leads to unbelievable joy among the people of God. Psalm 126:2. When life is brutal, joy is always possible. Luke 6:21. God will bring ultimate healing.

Those who call God as their Father see earthly suffering for what it is. Following Jesus turns pain into glory Confusion changes into wonder. Sin is redeemed.

We are called to sing, rejoice, laugh, and play. We know our Creator is working out the perfect plan. This holy plan ends with a wedding banquet because of our restoration and rest. The sovereign power gives us a sure hope. God's loving kindness empowers us to play with joyous freedom, even before the wedding banquet begins.

This feeling of hope surpasses anything. Joy plays!

Chapter Eleven

# Joy Sings!

Music is one of the predominate vehicles for experiencing joy through the sense of hearing. Music is universal. Music is described as moving. "Being moved" is one way of describing the experience we call feeling. This feeling connects us to memory. It brings emotion that is more than an emotion. Music is an auditory experience that brings positive feelings. Music reaches deep down inside us touching our souls.

From beginning to end, Holy Scripture is full of music and song. A musician, Jubal, is named in Genesis 4. Jubal was the father of all who play the harp and flute. Genesis 4:11. There is plenty of singing in heaven, we do not have to wait. Psalm 95:1, 98:1. Music is an encounter with the living God.

Music empowers and deeply moves us. Music does not demarginalize te Word of God. We encounter God through God's grace, love, and our faith in God. Romans 10:17. We could survive in faith without music. The Word of God is "the sword of the Spirit."

Joy is shared when a community of believers gather. As we sing, we notice that some don't know why we sing. In the Old Testament psalms were central for singing in worship. John Calvin declared there should be no other songs sung in church. To most people that's a narrow view.

When worship shifted from the temple to the synagogue in the New Testament, singing continued. The apostle Paul urged believers to sing psalms, hymns, and religious songs. Colossians 3:15-17, Ephesians 5:15-20. When something wonderful happens to us, we want to share the news. Joy sings! Joy praises God.

When we praise God, it is natural to sing as authentic humans. We are doing what God created us to do. Made in the image of God, we reflect the majesty and praise for the glory of our Creator. James 5:13. Singing is one powerful way to express our emotions. Feelings do not equate with an authentic encounter of a God kind. It is okay to be emotional about faith. Singing enables us to express emotions. It's one way we express our joy. Faithful people see the world from a different perspective than those who do not. Psalm 89:1. They know the "joyful sound." Psalm 89:15.

There are 150 canonized songs. Psalms are chanted, recited, and sung. They embrace our life's lows as well as highs. The psalm singers were intimate with the experiences and emotions. They were not for hiding one's lamp under a bushel. These songs elatedly celebrate success and achievement will pomp and circumstances. Israel's hymnists welcomed the vividness of human life. Psalms were written by many different people, including Psalm 89 composed by Ethan. Psalm 89 is intensely personal. This song is about God as the rock of our salvation and that God brings faithfulness in heaven.

An assumption of the psalter is that God responds to people in distress. God is gracious and merciful. God abounds in loving kindness in all times and with each generation. Exodus 4:6-7.

Some of the Psalms explode with joy. Others implore pain. Psalms 106 and 107 identify material circumstances that cause misery. Both of these long psalms open with the words, "Give thanks to the Lord for he is good; for his loving kindness endures forever." Psalm 106 focuses on the nation of Israel in its love affair with God. Psalm 107 looks beyond Israel to all humankind.

Psalm 106 scolds Israel for forgetting God. They need to honor he grace of God from which they have benefited. Psalm 106:3. The song asks Israel to return to its faith. This poet gives us a picture of the inner conflict of God about how to handle Israel. God is exasperated that divine compassion will overwhelm the hurt of being inflicted by the chosen people. Psalm 106:40-41.

The bottom line is that although Israel has forgotten God, God has full memory. Psalm 106:13, 21, 45. God's compassion prevails beyond righteous indignation. The song gives responsibility to those God loves for their bad choices. This psalmist urges us to lift our eyes beyond the dominant culture. This psalm depicts two senses of joy tat are tightly linked. The first discusses the spiritual roots of suffering to turn the readers' attention to the second sense of he joy of living in obedience to God. Psalm 106 is a self-examination for the people of Israel.

## Psalm 107

Israel is not mentioned in Psalm 107. This psalm encourages the people to expect divine rescue as they cry out and God responds in grace and love. Psalm 107:6, 13, 19, 28. God will give them attention. The message of how one responds to being saved and rescued is important. Psalm 107:8, 15, 21, 31.

God is our safety net. The writer of Psalm 107 is not interested in scolding people. This message is telling them how to live well with life's precariousness. Grace is offered to strangers. There is no shaming, no punishment, only care that speaks louder than most sermons.

## Spiritual Misery and Joy

If I were to try to include more psalms that relate to joy, I'd have to expand this book. When I wrote commentaries on the 150 psalms, it took four huge volumes to publish it. I will write of the joy in two psalms. Psalms 4 and 32 illustrate how the collapse and repair of relationships. Both examine distress caused by these relationships. Psalm 4 is a song about disrupted relationships. I plan to include a chapter in this book on the importance of relationships. Psalm 4 aims to help us to repair our disrupted relationships. The psalmist writes with a sad emotion as he views the faithlessness of his readers.

We know and express our love for God if we are first reminded of God's unconditional love for us. As we sing, we focus on this truth about love. I John 4:19. We approach God with both love and reverence.

## Psalm 4

Psalm 4 is a lamenting psalm. This prophetic song urges the faithful to speak out against the faithless. Psalm 4 is ambiguous, confusing. The hurried nature in the writing creates a frenzied atmosphere in eight brief verses. The second half of Psalm 4 suggests a manner that can repair the disrupted relationship.

## Psalm 32

Psalm 32 is a soliloquy hat uses one person's experience of inner joy to instruct others. This song is a staccato divided into sections. At the onset, this psalmist reveals the theme. Joy is the result of being forgiven. Psalm 32:1-2. The psalmist then sings his story. Psalm 32:3-5. Confession is needed for relief.

The sad songs are turned into glad songs of deliverance. Psalm 32:7. Luke 15:7. Moving from dejection to hope, the power of joy is realized. Horizontal relationships are repaired for a vertical relationship to be made whole.

Joy is a spiritual matter quite apart from circumstances alone. Psalm 32 illustrates the spiritual and non-circumstantial sense of misery as well as joy.

Psalmists were about to disclose the reality of life. The songs were filled both with sadness and joy. We pay attention to the words we sing. We are not singing to impress others. We are bringing glory to God. We use all kinds of instruments. In Psalm 150, we read about use of the lute, harp, trumpet, timbrel, pipe, strings, and loud clashing cymbals.

Based on the small samples of the Psalm, these songs, like our hymns today, enable us to appreciate well-being and joy. Distinctions between secular and sacred fade before the singer's embrace of concerns of God for the experience of joy. Joy sings!

Praise is not reduced to singing only. We sing to bless God's name. To sing is to declare the glory of God. Singing psalms of praise is commanded in the Word of God. Exodus 15:21, Psalm 147:1-7, Psalm 149:1, Zephaniah 3:14.

## Does music encourage joy?

Does music have anything to say about joy? The choral finale of Beethoven's Ninth Symphony with the words from Fredrich Schiller's poem "Ode to Joy" It has become an anthem for humanity to hear and sing. What does music communicate about joy? The power of music is its Joy or expressions of both positive and negative feelings.

The history, freedom, and experimentation in church music gives us insight in the use of jazz, electronic, and popular music. (John Killinger, *Leave It to the Spirit*, pp. 168-169.

The Ninth Symphony is about the pursuit of joy. Schiller's narrative ends with a perceived culture of joy. This joy is a humankind united in singing.

Joy is created from the chaos and is the goal of all. This creation narrative conceives joy as power.

The divine spark of joy in "Ode to Joy" which acts as rejection against what has been given. The music is a counterforce emerging from an ontology of violence. Joy as a violent power is articulated for reaction against evil.
Music is then accompanied by a militaristic noise in Turkish percussion. Beethoven invites the listener to hurtle through the heavens as a joyful believer. The power is portrayed as speed. This speed and transcendence of Beethovenian joy is put into words as the music gathers force.
At Beethoven's monument in Vienna, Austria, we become aware of the necessary tragedy behind the joy. His music is commingling joy with death. Joy requires an appetite for danger. It is part of the *jouissance*. Death immortalizes victorious resurrection.

During a phone call most businesses will tell us, "While you are waiting, would you like to hear classical, country or pop music. I always ask to hear classical music."
Classical music is the sound of heaven.

## Mozart

Wolfgang Amadeus Mozart gives us what Christian joy sounds like. Joy is the foundation of the meaning of his life. Mozart's music is pure play. His music affirms all creation in its total goodness.

Mozart created order for those who have ears to hear. Clement of Alexandria described Christ as the new song. The singing of the gospel retuned the fallen universe. Clement had a vision of music as the singing of the redeemed with Christ.

Mozart's "total music" was independent of life's circumstances. His music is rooted in the goodness of God and the fruit of the Spirit. It is fundamentally joy. Mozart was armed with the Word of God. No other of the great musicians before and after him, either knew or expressed as he did.

Mozart said that he was only an ear for the joy of the music and a communicator to other ears. Mozart believed God deserved praise. The Lord desires our whole-hearted praise.

Singing is a form of prayer. The Psalms show that God desires praise. Psalm 9:1, 86:12, 111:1, 138:1. These prayers were sung. Exhortations to sing Psalms include commands to sing prayers.

Singing plays a role to bridge the gap between the cognitive and affective aspects of our life journeys. The power of singing Psalms is immense. We are praying divinely inspired words.
When we are singing, we are also praying. Be aware that in singing, our body, mind, and soul are fully engaged. I Corinthians 14:15. If your church is in a spirit of joy, you might hear the music leader say, "Let us lift our voices together in prayer as we sing this next song."

Bach and Handel are highly lauded with most church people today. John Killinger wisely wrote, "The experience of the Christian is an experience in recreation, of newness, and of novelty. To limit the musical expression of that experience to traditional, approved, orthodox music is to saddle it immediately with a weight it cannot continue to bear. It must inevitably develop a lameness, and end in total paralysis." (John Killinger, op. cit., p. 171)

Most mainline churches repeat hymns, anthems, and cantatas from the past. Singing songs of the classic tradition, forbids contemporary and joyful expressions of faith. Younger musicians come to associate the church with dullness. My grandson Ethan Coffin who is majoring in music and mechanical engineering, would agree that if we are not free to uncover our identities today. In his studies at Lafayette College in Pennsylvania, he can play with sounds or colors or shapes.

Our spirits long to listen to the words of peace and hope. Christmas music bring on smiles with the words of cheer and joy. Church choirs sing with passion as we sense the uniqueness of the moments as Christ Jesus is born anew. The songs of Christmas become acts of joyous living that will be sustained beyond the advent season.

Church musicians have little understanding of the history of church music. Most congregations own a piano and an organ. Both instruments are newcomers for the church sanctuary. Choirs are carry-overs from monks who sang in the medieval church.
Ethan, my grandson, and college students today enjoy hearing ballads and creative singing of songs in worship. John Killinger asks his readers to consider Paul Simon's "The Sound of Silence," recounting ten thousand singers words "talking without speaking" and "hearing without listening.". John Killinger, Ibid., pp. 178-179).

We are now free to receive from the past what serves the vision of the present. Some liberal minds cannot bear to hear what is traditional. Conservative minds do not tend to tolerate unconventional singing. Musical instruments are accompaniments for the human voice.
"Religion is sung, whistled, stamped, danced, clapped, more than it is thought. There should exist a precarious balance between the two, but it is essential hat thought not prevail over the ability to vent the emotions rhythmically. (John Killinger, op. cit., p. 185.)

The Protestant Reformation included a desire to increase the participation of the congregation. Singing is way of encouragement. Ephesians 5:18-19. Our singing is addressed to God. Paul teaches it is also addressed to one another. Christians in the New Testament met together primarily to encourage each other. Colossians 3:16.

When we sing, we are not simply a collection of individual people praising God. Psalm 95:1, 3-4. We need to be built up in our faith and in faithfulness.

Music empowers us to embed words deeply into our minds and souls. Charles Wesley was obsessed by the writing of hymns. He did not preach often, nor was it he wrote theology books. Wesley's hymns are still sung to encourage Christians in our day.

Song writing should not be limited to those who are gifted musically. The best of the classic hymns, such as Charles Wesley's "And can it be," are filled with profound theology.

Morris Ashcraft, my professor of theology at Midwestern Baptist Theological Seminary in Kansas City, told his students, "Tell me the songs you sing, and I can tell what your theology is."

God-focused hymns bring encouragement and spiritual maturity. We should be able to use metaphor and imagery in our songs. Maturity and clarity does not mean dull singing. Some of our tunes sound dated now. The words are eternally true.

### The Joy of Easter Singing

Enjoying singing at Easter brings deep moments of joy. Easter singing shapes Christian culture. It has become a custom in many places to wear new clothes during the vigil of Easter.

I used to make the sermon following Easter, Low Sunday, with a humorous sermon to help people laugh after a somber Lent. It was the custom to tell jolly tales that were created to produce gaiety after the somber time.

Easter bells ring all day in many places after Easter. A bell choir is the order of the day. Easter incites a musical celebration. People who are filled with the joy of God will sing. Singing is a natural part of how Christians celebrate the resurrection. Ephesians 5:18-20.

Lutherans have a tradition of joyful singing throughout the year. Bach composed music for the Lutheran church in Leipzig. He captured in his music the essence of the great Christian feasts. He wrote Easter Oratorio in 1725. He reworked it during Easter. The music piece contrasts the unexpected joy of the resurrection with the disciples' grief reaction upon their mourning at the tomb of Jesus.

Laughter, joy, and power in the first duet was heard in the voices of the singers. In the center of the work, Mary proclaims to John and Peter that the angel announced that Christ has risen. They find the empty shroud. There is a wondrous reflection of how our own death will be gentle. The thought is surrounded with peaceful and soothing music. Then trumpets erupt with the voices of the choir to end on a note of exultant celebration.

White Christians enjoy singing hymns that came out of the black cultural experience. Songs with Aretha Franklin, Lena Horne, and so many others bring the joy of singing into church worship.

During and after the American Civil War, black slaves sang:

"Gonna lay down my sword and spear
Down by the riverside, down by the riverside,
Gonna lay down my sword and spear, Down by the riverside.

Oh I ain't going to study war no more, no more, Ain't gonna study war no more."

Slaves left plantations of the south and enlisted in the army of the north. This song was based on Isaiah 2:4. They used the words "down by the riverside" reminded them of the time they were baptized in the river when they became children of God.

I cherish the times in my ministry when I was privileged to baptize those professing and possessing Christ in a river. During one of my river baptism events, a woman who was not planning to be baptized, ran toward us and exclaimed, "I want to be baptized today."

Joy Sings to Inspire Black Empowerment

Black spirituals, blues, jazz, rock, and hip hop now enjoy global influence. Black music inspires all races. Songs that became freedom songs function as congregational songs. Black congregational songs are started by a song leader. She is different from a soloist. A song leader begins the singing. A soloist sings the whole song alone.

"This Little Light of Mine" was sung by black and whites, especially with the children. "We Shall Overcome" gives people an opportunity to pour into sound of singing voices and commitment to the freedom struggle.

When people sing about nonviolence, they think about passive or peaceful singing. Blacks joyfully sang "Onward Christian Soldiers" in their churches. Black folks chose to leave their obedience to segregation to go where they might lose everything. People celebrated by coming together to sing "What a Fellowship, What a Joy Divine."

None of the texts were changed. "We Shall Not Be Moved" was another empowering song. When many blacks sang, you could hear them a block away. We walked in the sound of the voice.

Most of the singing was church songs. Younger blacks brought additional genres of music with fewer hymns and more gospel music and concert spirituals, and new songs. Young people sang with full power. Singing helped fear to disappear. Joy sings!

## Country Music

Country music has a long and rich history. Two famed Christian music producers were in my McReynolds' family tree: Jim and Jesse McReynolds from Southwest Virginia. Joy sings! Country music has become an effective for rejoicing and sharing faith.

Southern country music is quite popular in the southern states. There is something for every country music fan. In my youth and childhood, singing country songs was the usual part of worship.

When I accepted the call as pastor of the First Christian Church of Weeping Water, Nebraska, singing country music and entertaining guest artists became a way to become a growing church.

The Blackwood Brothers were quite popular. They were from Shenandoah, Iowa. They made records and performed throughout the country, especially the Midwest. I enjoyed the joy of seeing more than 500 people almost every Saturday night singing with the country singers.

One of my joys was serving them for almost 11 years and baptizing 100 people into the church. We hosted many famous singing stars.

Randy Travis is a prominent country music and gospel music artist. He is known for his traditional country sound and deep baritone voice. He has sung in the largest churches in the nation.

Carrie Underwood, an all-time Grammy Award winner, was never shy about her faith. Her faith took root in her Christian family church in Oklahoma. Her song, "Jesus, Take the Wheel" was sung to millions. She has sold more than 90 million records.

Gary Chapman is a contemporary Christian singer. He gave concerts with two gospel groups, the Downings and the Rambos. The famed singer Amy Grant was married to Chapman for 17 years. She divorced him to marry another famed singer.

Tennessee Ernie Ford was from my hometown, Bristol, Tennessee. He was a beloved singer and often sang in his home church, the Anderson Street United Methodist Church in Bristol.

The singer credited with commercializing gospel Christian music was Susan Ashton. She became popular throughout the world at a time, the 1990s, when the market was flourishing. Ashton began singing at the age of seven in church choirs and talent shows. She was well known by the time she was in high school. She discovered the kind of music she wanted to pursue was contemporary country gospel music.

Joy sings! Classical, jazz, popular, or country gospel has been a source of joy for generations, sharing the gospel with the word. Throughout the history of music church historians have communicated about the existence of Christian styles of music.

Paul writes of "addressing one another in psalms and hymns and spiritual songs." Colossians 3:15-17. Paul and the early Christians taught that singing is integral to the spiritual life and health of the congregation.

The songs we sing are remembered long after our sermons have been forgotten.

Joy sings!

# Chapter Twelve

# Joy Shares!

Life is a place of service. Joy comes as we visualize life as a service. Joy shares! When we are born so helpless, our service is giving our parents joy and making them feel proud. At the other end of life, when we are on our deathbed, we can't share our joy.

Discussing our joy experiences leads to more energy, increased well- being, and overall life satisfaction. Charlotte Bronte wrote, "Joy quite shared can scarcely be called joy." People sharing joy with someone on any given day, the more satisfied they are on that same day. They had more vitality and zest for life.

We share our faith and joy to spread God's fame. We exist to bring glory to God. When people know Jesus, the glory of God is known and shown. II Corinthians 4:5-6. Hope is needed. Ephesians 2:1, 4-5, 12.

Joyful people share because they speak for God. God trusts us with the privilege of being ambassadors for Christ. II Corinthians 5:18-20. Ministers, joyologists, professing Christians of all kinds are honored as God's ambassadors.

We are never responsible to save. We are asked to share. The end result is up to God. We can share our spiritual autobiography, the story about how God saved by grace and love. It is a story that is unique to you. No one can debate or discuss the validity. Jesus made himself real to you and you fully believed it.

No one's testimony is better or more interesting than any other person. The final scene is the same. We can speak on how we were saved from death toward the joy of God's kingdom. Tell how your life was like before you came to Christ. Share honestly your struggle, your personal circumstances, and the questions you had.

Tell how Christ changed you. How you are different from when you were lost in sin. Be up to date and share what God is doing in your life today. Share what God is doing now.

The author of I John wrote to make our joy complete. I John 1:4. As we enjoy our relationship with Christ, we can't help but desire that others become a part of the community of God's love and grace. Joy shares!

We can learn from Jesus and his way of asking good questions. Sharing conversations with people is informing. Pray for opportunities to share each day. The opportunities will come in surprising ways.

Sharing requires preparation. We gather resources to pass on to others. Joyful refreshment comes from drawing from the well of our salvation.

Sharing joy brings difficulty. Working hard for decades and experiencing the difficulties of broken relationships, illness, setbacks, and all the things involved in living. Life is joy shared. Life is a place of service. Service is joy.
When we understand our lives are services, we find we want to support and protect those we love. To have no one in this life to serve is to have no life. Lasting joy comes from serving others. To know how to live in any relationship requires service.

Joy is the elixir of life. Christ's disciples follow his lead and serve one another. Jesus promised that those who serve others would be blessed. John 13:15-17. Those who jumpstart our joy will likely be the ones who support us. They give us constructive, enthusiastic, positive and encouraging messages. When we share our joy, we select someone be a supportive listener. Sharing joy increases joy.

The Holy Bible teaches divine reciprocity. Planting seeds of loving service reaps a harvest of blessings. Proverbs 11:25. Joy increases as we serve. We share the connection with others. When we invest our lives in serving others and loving them like Jesus does. Joy increases connections and feelings of joy.

The apostle Paul reminds us that each human is a unique poem written by God, designed to do good works that God has ordained. Ephesians 2:10. God gives us strengths and grace intended for service to others. No one act of service is greater than another. The key to finding joy in service to others is to serve people our of your own gifts.

When we feel our joy slipping, ask God to give you renewed joy as you keep on serving. Jesus hears our prayer. Matthew 7:7. Jesus wants us to be filled with joy when we are serving others.

## Sharing a Meal

In the New Testament when someone is transformed and reconciled to God because of Jesus, hey celebrate with a joyful meal. After leaving his tax office, Levi gives a banquet for Jesus. Luke 5:27-30. When the Philippian jailer is saved, he becomes filled with joy. He brings Paul and Silas into his home for a meal. Acts 16:31-34. Zacchaeus welcomed Jesus into his home. Luke 19:5-7.

Sharing the experience of salvation with as many friends, families, and neighbors is in the New Testament account with an invitation for a meal. Joy shares! Joy celebrates! When someone is saved from sin there is an outpouring of joy. People open their homes as they come to meet Jesus. Jesus is infectious. Sharing Christ has a snowballing effect.

Sharing their stories was a normal response in the New Testament. II Corinthians 5:14-21. Evangelism is not just a chore for Christians, it's the joy of sharing our homes, our meals, time, words, and lives with as many people as possible. There is bountiful joy in enjoying living as a new person in Christ. Once we have tasted this joy; we want the whole world to taste it as well. God will put people on our paths to encounter people in light of eternity. Evangelism is simply sharing the Good News. This love sharing is as natural to a Christian committed to Christ as breathing. We need a heart for sharing. Sharing our faith is as natural and second nature as breathing in and out.

God's ways are not our ways, and our ways are not God's ways. We need to eliminate our preconceived notions. Kindness does a long way. Read my recent book on the power of kindness.

## The Joy of Evangelism

As disciples of Jesus Christ, we are ambassadors for Christ becoming fishers of men and women and disciple makers. Sharing the joy of our faith and our faithfulness leads others to Christ.

Each person's journey is different. Each day we encounter people that only we will meet and with whom we interact. Joy shares!

In my book, *The Joy of Preaching: Encountering Jesus through the Word of God,* I share the incredible love I have for preaching. Harold Bales and I were friends for 40 years. Harold and I were in the classes from 1968- 1972 at Vanderbilt University Divinity

School. We both shared our joy and lived and worked in Nashville. Harold served the Methodist Board of Evangelism and I served at the Sunday School Board of the Southern Baptist Convention.

My book on preaching was dedicated to everyone who had heard my preaching and responded to the Word of God. One of my English professors at Carson-Newman University greatly encouraged me when she told me that I had "a poetic soul, a gift of working language into something beautiful and meaningful." The joy of preaching cannot be limited to Sundays in a local church sanctuary.

Evangelism and preaching are held together as we re-think church. I have preached on more than 5,000 campus settings, in prisons and county jails, in hospital chapels, for community groups, nursing homes and care center chapels, for high school baccalaureates and Youth for Christ, Young Life, summer youth camps, and wherever people gather.

Be ready to defend the faith. If you have a large home, you can use it to share the Good News. We are commanded to love others. Explain the reason why there is hope. Joy hopes!

## The Joy of Sharing Joy

There is no greater joy in the preaching life than to discover that embracing the call to preach has placed us in a special relationship with God. God's Word brought everything into existence. Jeremiah says that God knew us before we were born. God decided to place us in this world.

The preacher awakens spiritual life if she is sensitive to the Holy Spirit in awareness of joy and the sharing of joy. Witnessing has no cookie-cutter approach. We can know for certain that when people profess their faith, they become part of God's family. They receive all of God, including the Holy Spirit, who now dwells in them.

126

Sharing positive experiences leads to more energy, life satisfaction, and well-being. Sharing joy with close friends and romantic ones is important. Making gratitude lists draws attention to the joy experiences and improves our health. Gratitude improves our connections with other people.

Those who talk to people that close with about the good that is happening in their lives experience more times of joy. People who are close to us are more like to support us. Receiving enthusiastic, positive, and encouraging thoughts after a successful moment will give us appreciation and love.

Joy shares! The bottom line is sharing joy increases joy. We can support other people's joy by encouraging them to share their joy. This deep sharing impacts not only ourselves, but the joyful connection to that friend.

Albert Schweitzer, a German physician, musician, and joy spotter who won the Nobel Peace Prize, declared, "Joy is the only thing that multiplies when you share it."

Joy exists in relation to a specific person, object, or encounter. Joy, like love, is shared. Joy originates as a dimension of the family of God. Love is positively joyous.

The Christian church encounters love in how it worships. Good News is shared out of a surplus of love. John 10:10. We gather to offer God gratitude and thanksgiving.

The joy of the Lord is more than a momentary feeling. Christian joy is an affection, a disposition of the soul. Joy is desiring the kingdom with hope. Our human pump is primed for joy. John 1:43-51.

Times of experiencing sheer joy is found in working language into something good, meaningful, and beautiful. Joy is found in fulfillment of the anticipation of helping bring joy into the people we love. Jesus challenged his listeners to a conversion of life that means setting aside things that keep people from embracing Jesus.

The joy of self-transcendence comes as we participate in music groups, sports teams, church staffs, or a number of cooperative groupings. These cooperative groups create a power or feeling that one is living beyond themselves. We live in the joy zone together.

The human expression of joy springs out the affective flavor of remembered joy. Joy is the gift of overflowing love from God. As minister of joy sharing the distinction between using the world and enjoying God. We must be willing to be willing.

Preachers continue to capture and re-capture the joys of preaching when we prayerfully return to what has happened with us personally. I Corinthians 9:19-23. Salvation comes from the grace and love of God. God opens our mouths to exhale the saving Good News. The only failure in witnessing is not speaking up and sharing your faith. I share with unbelievers why I am better than I deserve.

Of course, I am concerned about outcomes. I really am not possessed by them. We all need to hone our skills, so I do a better job of sharing our faith. The outcome does not depend on me. It depends on the mercy of God. Be prepared to share. I Peter 3:15.

After a baptism service, the pastor might say, "They come by their profession of faith." It is an appropriate way to describe one's standing with Jesus. Profession of faith may not be the same as "possession of faith." In all our faithful churches, new members have walked the aisle, talked to a counselor or another seasoned church member welcomes them and prays with them. We are certainly not to judge, but some professions of faith does not mean possession of faith. John 8:31-32.

Jesus told us that not everyone who professes faith shall enter the kingdom of Heaven. Matthew 7:21. Emotions are involved when we receive Jesus. Faith and faithfulness overshadow it all.

Gentleness and respect season each moment we share. We share with the joy and love of Jesus in our hearts. Being available for God's use is essential.

When we go to heaven, an angel or God might ask us, "Did you enjoy your journey through the world?"

Churches are holding kingdom parties. Congregations are preparing ultimate feasts of the kingdom of God. Hospitality is extended to every person.

The needy ones are invited. Worshipping God with the needy ones means all of us who have responded to the Word of God.

And that is the joy of preaching. Joy shares.

How you share your salvation story may be unique. The most important thing is that you ae willing to share your faith. Sharing faith is evidence of how important your faith is to you.

A witness is someone who has observed, heard, and experienced something they now share. Witnessing is the telling of what Jesus did for us. We implore people to embrace Jesus.

Within our Christian journey, nothing excites us more than letting all those people you will encounter will know the difference God makes and how true life is found in Jesus. Nothing is like the joy of being part of someone choosing to take hold of eternal life.

We must look and sound like Jesus. That is why God has us living on the earth. Becoming like Jesus makes it possible to influence as many family, friends, and neighbors to join us. Supporting another's positive experiences of joy impacts not only ourselves, but those that are all around us.

Joy shares!

Chapter Thirteen

# Joy Enjoys!

Enjoying what we love to do empowers us to feel alive inside. Filling our lives with things that we enjoy has a huge impact on the joy we feel. In my ministry practices, I ask people to tell me what they love.

As a joyologist, or one who shares joy, I have discovered that part of the problem is that we don't give ourselves time and space to identify the things that we enjoy.

Think back to your own childhood. Recall the joy of playing with children, your grandkids, or kids at church. Without pressure from outside world, what did you enjoy? What games did you play? Did you enjoy coloring and reading books?

And just like children, adults need to play. To enjoy joy, we need to do some things just because we want to. Tap into the new things that you love but have not become into our awareness.

## Fun in Our Jobs

As long as we have fun in our work, it shows. Fun is infectious. We make it a joyful experience.

What would your dream day look like? Enjoying God sounds too good to be true. God wants us to enjoy life. Psalm 16:11. Joy is the enjoyment of God and the love, grace, and joy that comes from the hand of God.

Enjoying joy sums up the essentials of joy. Joy is a derived term of enjoy. Enjoy is to receive pleasure. Joy is to feel an emotion. Joy rejoices! Enjoy is a verb that means to receive pleasure or satisfaction. Nehemiah encourages his weary fellow workers with the words "the joy of the Lord is my strength."

Enjoyment and Joy

Joy is intense and especially ecstatic. The feeling is an intense pleasure. Joy is the expression of that feeling. Joy feels like extreme cheerfulness because of the expectation of something good.

Enjoyment is the use or possession of something beneficial. It is the condition of enjoying anything. Enjoyment gives keen satisfaction. Enjoyment is the pleasure felt when we are experiencing a good time. Enjoyment is hope of everlasting and eternal enjoyments. It is an enjoyable state of mind.

Joy includes to enjoy. Joy gladdens. Joy exhilarates. Joy is a positive outcome. Joy is a child's response on a Christmas morning. Joy is a delight of the mind in the present. Joy exhibits merriment, festivity, and mirth.

Most of us are searching for joy. We discover joy when we find purpose and meaning in life. We find joy in families who support and love us. We live in life and work through enjoyment of our journey together. Fresh insight from the Word of God. God longs to give us exceeding joy. Psalm 43:4. God's desire for us is beyond imagination. We can barely contain outbursts of praise, adoration, and gratitude. God delights in these unplanned moments.

The French use *jouissance* for enjoying sexual intercourse. Joy is intense and ecstatic, or an instance of a deep feeling.

Enjoy means to have use or benefit, like enjoying good health. Joy is the expression of such feeling. To enjoy is to have pleasurable or satisfactory time.

Enjoy is he source or an abject of joy such as an only child, a pride and joy. We enjoy holidays. Some holidays are remembered as joyful times. Christmas, Easter, birthdays, anniversaries or certain July fourths.

Enjoying football is what millions do. Winning in a football game brings joy to those who are the winners of the games. Joy is cheerfulness, especially related to the acquisition or expectation about something good.

Enjoy is to take pleasure and feel delighted as to enjoy the dainties of a feast. One of the best meals that I remember from long ago was one I ate in Columbia, Missouri. That meal became a joy.

Enjoy is deriving or receiving pleasure in as "she relished her fame and basked in her glory." Norman Vincent Peale said, "If you are not getting as much from life as you want to, then examine the state of your enthusiasm." Joy enjoys with a positive disposition. Enthusiasm means having God within. Joy fills us with life, light, and the love of God.

Joy enliven our spirits and makes our eyes sparkle. Enjoying our joys connects with "the joy of the Lord" to make us feel peaceful, excited, and exciting at the same time. Feel alive. Feel passion. Lighten up. Reframe.

Our children and grandchildren ply, sing, laugh, and dance with joy. Feel God. We were inspired as children with activities we enjoyed. Teach things that you enjoy, and enthusiasm will appear and grow in your journeys.

Special people are joy igniters. Igniting joy will fire up imagination and enthusiasm. Joy celebrates every moment. Celebrate in small ways just by feeling good and enjoying that feeling.

Smile with joy. Enjoying the joy is to smile and sing. Remember the popular song, "When you smile, the whole word smiles at you." We smile when a baby or a child smiles at us. Smiles radiate out of a cheerful heart. Eyes sparkle and the whole face looks full of joy.

Enjoying joy is seeing miracles wherever we look. I enjoy bumblebees. Engineers inform us that bumblebees cannot fly. Laws of aerodynamics proves that they cannot fly.

Keep yourself joyful and share your joy. We will live longer, and friends and family will want you to be around. All of us has shared something exciting to us, but that other person did not respond, but criticized our jubilation, and left us deflated. Being deflated is a huge part of the reality of life for many people. Nobody is except from all sorts of disappointments.

Face Difficulties with Joy

I think it was my friend John Killinger who shared the old story of two little boys during Christmas. One boy was a joyless pessimist. The other eluded joy and was an optimist.

Each boy woke up that morning and raced downstairs. They wanted to see what presents Santa Claus brought them.

The joyless pessimistic child saw a huge pile of manure and expressed his utter disgust. He told his family, "Well, I knew that I was not going to get anything good." Killinger might have added that the pessimist just blew up his balloon and ate his orange, and Christmas was over for him."

The optimistic boy saw the manure. This son and brother excitedly and enthusiastically dived into the manure pile. The parents ask him what he was doing. The joyful optimist answered, "With all this horse manure, there has to be a pony for me."

Those two boys chose differing responses to the same situation. Both boys had a choice to react on Christmas morning. We can reach our life goals in facing every difficulty with joyous enthusiasm.

Scripture informs us seven times to be of good cheer. It does not tell us to be of good cheer only in good times. Realize that God is with us all the time. Enjoy the courage of not being alone. We can be that little boy in the Christmas story and be disappointed. Se we will walk away from the pile of manure or like the other boy, we can with enthusiastic passion dive in and look for the gift hidden there.

During one of my visits to see my grandson, I observed him playing around the goodies table at his mom's wedding. When he saw me, his eyes lit up as he yelled, "Grandpa Jim," with enthusiastic, exciting, unbridled joy.

We humans have a bad habit of wanting things that end up being terrible for us. An abundance of refined sugar rots our teeth. Sugar blows out our immune system. Avoiding exercise weakens our bones and joints and causes depression. People are wired to relax and seek tasty things, because until recent times, humans were more likely to survive and pass on their genes if they got more calories and were under less physical strain.

The Desire for Fame

An example of this mismatch between what we want and what nourishes us is our desire for fame. In our culture, a person is successful if they are rich, have a high-profile career, or are ell known. When I was a pastor, I continuously saw people wave or speak to me who otherwise would ignore me. Fame is not a route to joy. Fame militates against the ingredients of well-being.

Assuming my readers are not a president or a senator, or a pop star, fame appears as an abstract problem. Fame is a relative thing. So is prestige. Fame among a group of people is just as fervently chased in smaller communities and in fields of our expertise.

Being known and admired makes us more likely to attract a lover or a mate. We enjoy finding that thousands of years ago, our 30th great grandfather or grandmother was a king or queen.

People want to be famous in order to be seen and valued, even by complete strangers. Folks desire an elite, high-status lifestyle. Billy Graham enjoyed more fame than any other preacher in history. He was buried with honors from the White House. His funeral was broadcast throughout the world. By contest, some unknown poor pastor in Belch Lake, Kentucky was buried with no attendants tohis celebration of life.

Even if a person's motive for fame is to set a positive example, it mirrors the other, less flattering moves insofar as it depends on other people's opinions. Fame is not found within ourselves. Fame is based on what historians call extrinsic rewards.

Fame became an addiction with rulers and dictators such as Hitler, Stalin, and all those e still read about in history or on television. We see the addiction to fame on social media. Fame has become like saltwater, "The more we have, the thirstier we become." Lady Gaga told us, "Fame is a prison."
Seeking fame is a glitch in finding joy. Fame promises contentment but delivers misery. Look closely at your motivations. If your motives for doing anything are more fame based than you will admit, consider the value that doing it would bring relative to the high cost.

136

People will find all your bosting annoying. Famous people call themselves "humble." Imagine people whom you don't know forming an opinion about your looks, your personality, or your work. Possibly the way you make your living offers you no way around spending millions to attract attention to yourself.

Stand up for yourself. Do not brag or seek attention. Delete all your postings and take a social media break. Connect to someone who loves you for who you are, not just for the things you hope somebody might admire or envy.
Emily Dickinson, the American poet, wrote that fame is "a fickle food upon a shifting plate." Joy enjoys! Enjoy your joys that God gives to us freely. Joys come as a surprise. Nobody can create joy. It is a fruit of the Holy Spirit.

Most people have nothing written about themselves on their gravestones. Most have just a dash between two dates, the birth date and the death date. If I have a choice I'd enjoy the words, "Minister of Joy to the World." That is not a desire for fame, but a statement of our purpose and fulfillment in our journey.

We are not living to impress, but to delight. Emotions are not isolated or singular. They are connected and build on each other, just like the fruit of the Spirit. The benefits we discover from one single joy experience sets us up for more joy now and in the future. Joy creates more joy.

Joy enjoys!

# Chapter Fourteen

# Joy Lasts!

Eternal joy is not a temporary joy only experienced in a day. Joy lasts. Eternal joy transcends each day and each year of our lives. The lasting joy we will experience in heaven will emanate from God.

While we are here on earth, we experience part of the eternal joy that God in Christ will give us. Those who have the Holy Spirit indwelling in our souls, are drawn to love, grace, and joy. The Bible tells us what heavenly joy will be like when we are living in heaven. Isaiah 51:11.
The Psalms give the writer anticipation of being in the presence of God's joy. Palm 84:1-3. Revelation 21:3-4 gives us a glimpse of the joys we will experience in heaven.

As we look to that time, we need to be prepared with salvation in our hearts. We need to walk with God every single day. Matthew 6:19-20.

As we live each day, we anticipate the eternal joy that we will experience in heaven with that hope bring joy into our everyday life now.

The Men's College World Series in Omaha gave lasting joy to the teams who won the NCAA championship. The joy was more like the ideal emotional experience with intense, manic euphoria. Excitement is necessary. Life would not be fulfilled without it. Peak experiences can bring false joy. A 90-year-old man clearly remembered when he played on the College World Series back In 1955. His joy, he said, will never end.

Gift recipients or lottery winners scream, hyperventilate, and shake. Even the highest excitement is followed by a mood crash. Some even feel lifeless and depressed.

Joy lasts forever. The joy of heaven is beyond our comprehension. I Corinthians 2:3. Humans have attempted to communicate their inklings of joy in heaven. Heavenly joy is much greater than anything we have experienced on earth. All joys are the enjoyment of God. James 1:17. Where God is not enjoyed, nothing is enjoyed. The divine excellence of joy in heaven will be known at last. Not just in part or indirectly, but in our means of grace and one day we will enjoy God in glory face to face. I Corinthians 13:12.

Joy in heaven will exceed those known on earth. Eternal joy will not fade. Earthly joy is limited and fading, but forever joy is endless. Here our pleasures fade. We humans age and decay. There where death does not exist, our joy goes on without interruption. To enjoy the life journey is immortal bliss.

The joys of heaven will be always fresh. Every element of joy will be there. This is the quintessence of joy. God will be glorified fully in the coming kingdom. The long history of the world is a grand symphony where all clashing conflict will forever be resolved, and every disharmony is finally laid to rest.

Life's Brief Moments and Eternity

Our responsibility is to use our temporal life span to create a just and joyful community for our generation and for our children. Life on earth is but a few brief moments in comparison with eternity.

Eternity thinking charges this life with enormous significance. Eternity magnifies the importance of our choices. Knowing the way to heaven is important. That knowledge is crucial for his life to be meaningful. Life is meaningless without a hereafter.

Listen to the lasting words of Robert Browning: "Grow old along with me! The best is yet to be. The last of life, for which the first was made. Our times are in God's hands." Understanding that concept lies in the beliefs concerning eternity, incarnation, meaning, and revelation that only makes sense with emphasis on heaven. Joy lasts! Eternity in heaven has resilience and staying power. Heaven has been conceived in varieties images; it is understood with identifiable features. Some have viewed heaven as a timeless experience of infinity and the reality of God. We will receive the fullness of joy.

The Book of Revelation has been interpreted in fanciful and fanatical words. Heaven is visualized as a community of people who have been transformed by the love of God. There is general agreement among writers that the joy of heaven is the joy of salvation. Salvation is loving God and having a relationship which is the source of deepest delight.
Heaven is not a place that could be enjoyed apart from loving God in the way made possible by salvation. This consensus among writers about heaven and salvation reflects our ideas about salvation.

## Salvation by the Grace of God

Salvation is enabled by the grace of God. We cannot reform or save ourselves with our own efforts. The perfect life of Christ is appropriate reparation because it represents the kind of life we should have lived.

This act of pleading the atonement involves a change of heart that will eventually, with God's grace, bring spiritual transformation. This involves a transforming relationship with Christ and his body, the church. Just as a child comes to share the character of her family, believes share the character of Christ.

Salvation requires belief in Jesus' deity. Salvation is about a perfect relationship with God. Belief in Christ is an honest response to divinely disclosed reality. Saving faith is the opposite of sin, so we must eliminate sin from our lives. Sin is mistrust of God or from ingratitude for God's love. We must recognize God's perfect wisdom and unbounded love for us. We are changed so that we gladly love and obey God.

We are united in mutual love. God has always loved us, but we have not always loved God. The essence of salvation is the transformation that allows us to love God. The aim of salvation and the essence of heaven is restoration. When the climax of this precious relationship arrives, God and our faithfulness lasts until the end.

All my readers have attended church funerals in which the deceased who were hardly suspected of sainthood were declared to be enjoying heaven. We realize that these celebrations are efforts to comfort grieving loved ones. To hold on to sin, hatred, anger, or indignation destroys joy. Forgiveness and redemption are required. The doctrine of heaven is concerning eternal transforming grace. It is the only alternative for cruel suffering.

If we can look with the eyes of faith, claiming God's eternal promises, we can take what comes at any moment. Joy lasts! We face each day with courage. We live content to let be what will be. God gives us the power to dream about tomorrow.

Life might have been good, but we desire only what heaven can provide. Our need for God is an important part of the structure of our every desire. We must face the harm that came from the journey through a fallen word.

Life will not work apart from God. The joy of rich involvement with another human being is much greater than the risk of being rebuffed.

I always enjoyed going to camps and conference centers as a youth. I think I enjoyed it even more when I spent four summers at Ridgecrest Conference Center in North Carolina. People in pain do want to talk. We all want a future different from our past. We see with enlightened and differing eyes. We must not live in the past or the future but be alive now. Few people whom I have encountered and shared their story have ever said, "And now what?"

We must live in eternity. Our eternity is rushing toward us. We will never be able to predict our last day on earth. We exist in the light of an eternity streaking toward us. Death comes on a day that only God knows for sure.

## The Teaching About Heaven

Constructive teaching about heaven offers the only realistic way of restructuring our lives and reinterpreting our past history for a hopeful, lasting future. Only a teaching about salvation that represents the satisfaction of our deepest longing for joy holds promise hat earthly suffering will pale in comparison.

The desire for assurance of eternal life and immortality underlies teachings about heaven. Teaching about heaven reviews the distinctive human reflections on the meaning of life. Human beings do not discover joy by accomplishing things in our earthly living. We do not delight in pushing our stones repeatedly up our hills, never stopping to ask why.

We are born with an instinctive will to live in heaven forever. We are blissfully indifferent to questions of deeper meaning and satisfaction. The Christian teaching holds out the hope of unending joy and fulfillment.

The doctrine about heaven implies that we were intended to exist, and we were created for flourishing, not extinction in he death of the solar system. Our creator is essentially a God of love God desires the fulfillment of all that has been created. God exists in three persons in an eternal relationship of perfect love. We are taught that even though we are fallen and estranged from God apart from grace, we were created in the image of one whose character is love. God's creative purpose was to have a lasting relationship.

When we receive or witness love, we are drawn to it because it is a foretaste of the eternal joy. The lasting love of God is both a gift and a reception. Christian teaching provides intelligible and persuasive accounts of how moral obligation has an objective and transcendent foundation. This teaching mirrors reality that we are related by creation to a personal God. It provides powerful resources to resolve dilemmas that have plagued us for centuries.

John Keats wrote, "A thing of beauty lasts forever." His line can be interpreted as "a beautiful thing will give joy throughout a person's lifetime. As we return to any beautiful thing, it will never cease to be a source of joy.

Richard of Chichester wrote a prayer and hymn that was always fitting for summer assemblies. "Day by day, dear Lord, of three things I pray. To see Thee more clearly, Love Thee more dearly, Follow Thee more nearly, Day by day."

Even after one dies, a thing of beauty will continue to exist. Beauty will give joy to people who will live in the next generation. As life goes and ends, the beauty gives joy to the next generation and the next. Joy lasts!

Because people share the same nature, they respond to stimuli in the same ways. Should a thing of beauty be lost even for centuries, we can have the ability to give joy to future generations, even if the Holy Spirit helps humans to rediscover what was lost.

Moments of joy have an impact that reaches beyond the moment of joy. Experiences of joy add more to life than the sum of its parts. Joy lasts!

Joy absorbs us in the present moment of time. Our senses are engaged when we focus of what is occurring now. Joy enables us to do this. We will know a more open views of the world. Flexibility in our thinking and deeper exploration in our behavior will be the result.

Joy compounds joy. A virtuous circle happens. Joyful people are less likely to be negative and they bounce back from anything life gives them. Joy sparks a big reaction. Finding joy is not work. It's fun.

We believe if we get enough material abundance, joy will come. But it will not last. Some people are forever searching for joy, but they never get to feel joyfulness in their pursuit. Joyfulness is available despite our circumstances.

We don't go out and reach for joy. We really can never hunt for it. We turn to God and embrace it. Joylessness is like the air we breathe. Air as joy is always there. Breathe joy into your heart. When my brother-in-law reached the age of 90, he was asked what his living secret was. "Keep breathing," he answered.

We tune in to the Holy Spirit as joy is always available, because we find it everywhere. We need to simplify our lives. Listen to the sound and songs of birds. Watch the drenching rain. See the branches on trees dancing with the wind.

## A Woman's Search for Joy

A woman named Kristine wondered the earth searching for the essence of joy. Nothing fulfilled her quest. Her time on earth came to an end. She was standing before a golden gate that led to the throne of God. She hesitated, questioning if she was worthy to enter. Eventually, she stood in front of the throne of God. Kristine was overwhelmed by the sheer power of God.

God gave her words of welcome. She then said to God, "I have been searching for joy my entire life. I have traveled far and wide, read numerous books, but I found nothing that brought me lasting joy." God told her joy can only be found in God. Ordinary people find that they are full of well-being, a calmer nervous system, and happiness in our longsuffering.

When joy feels far away, remember some little things. Noticing a scent that reminds you of someone you loved. Enjoying a sunset. These are small moments, but they are so moving. There more than enough joy

She remembered that her life lives in dawn, not in the night. She realized hat her life was not as bad as it could be. We never deserve what we have received. God is for Kristine and for us all demonstrated that when we were sinners, Christ died for us. Katherine became willing to push through her present trials in hope for lasting, untainted, unrestrained joy.

For many days, Kristine basked in the presence of God, soaking up the love and warmth. She found contentment in simply being with God. Lasting joy is not something that can be bought or earned.

She bathed in the radiance of the love of God. She realized that she found what he had been searching for all her life. Kristine would never be alone again. She would spend eternity in her creator's presence. Nothing would ever separate her from this love. (Sermon delivered at Central Baptist Church, Maysville, Kentucky and published by the congregation.)

The glory of God are humans being fully alive. Kristine and ourselves can look forward to meeting God who will give lasting joy.

Profound enjoyment or serious enjoying joy is our call to stop striving against the providence of God, and to trust that God is in control. The joy of the Lord lasts forever. Turn your eyes toward God in Christ Jesus, resting in divine purposes, and delighting in the eternal Christ and our disfigured world. By this lasting joy, we will find lasting gain unto eternity.

God values joy as the way to walk throughout our life journeys. Negative emotions are temporary. Joy will last forever. Joy is always present to empower us to overcome. Joy is a tangible light that lasts. Exultation increase revelation. Revelation exposes every situation to the will of God. Difficulties are changed into blessings, grace, and benediction. Joy overturns everything that is against us. Joy is resistance against domination. Joy does not float. It is entangled with eternity. Joy enables us to endure the contradictions of life.

Learn from each experience. Joy finds passion in simple things. Connect with joy. Relax. You don't have to pursue it or chase it.

The body of Christ illuminates these entanglements and complexities and gives new possibilities for joy. To find joy requires resisting that which leads to despair without hope.

Joy sings! Music and joy share a long history. Music is a lasting womb for joy. Music will forever live and breathe. Music takes flight through sound.

Joy work is communal as the pace on our planet is shared space. Hebrews 12:2. Joy overcomes social fragmentation and racism. The possibility of joy joins people who would never imagine that their joy together. Joy lasts through the brutality of social life.

We are given the opportunity of linking joy in ways only limited by our imagination and vision. Jesus speaks of a joy that gathers. The joy of the Lord gets its strength from the cloud of witnesses to the faithfulness of God.

Joy draws life from the life of God. The joy of living with God marks the life of God's family. John 15:8-13. We participate in the joy of Jesus as we are drawn into Christ's life for the lasting benefit of others. Shared joy has global dimensions.

A shared conversion brings common ecstasy as it moves through boundaries and overcomes fragmentation. Joy that is shared is issued in the commitment to love one another. Joy that gathers ends in the command to love.

That immortal love includes the people who live and love with us now and the eternal love of heaven. Words are powerful but divine joy goes beyond the experiences of joy we have ever known.

Joseph Campbell said, "Eternity has nothing to do with life. This is it. Heaven is not the place to have these experiences." John 10:10 is often misinterpreted.

Eternity Starts Now

We think of heaven or the kingdom of God as a place out there. Eternity starts in the now. We are circumscribed by our own immortality. We carry the seeds of our death. Heaven is a relationship between us and God. The Bible speaks of the now and the future. The future is determined in the now. Hope for the future is the faithfulness of the promises of God. Because God loves now, God will love us through all eternity.

Eternal life has already begun in the now. The promise of the future began in the now. The promise for the future is within the now. We can know nothing of the future life except as we imperfectly but really experience our life journey in the now of our present existence. Our history ends at our time of death.

Eternal life is given to human beings since it belongs only to God. Eternity can only be derived from the experience of the divine love. Salvation starts in history but transcends it. Salvation involves interpersonal communion with God. John 6:47-51.

Seeking lasting joy is to become clear on what it means to follow Jesus. Following Christ brings us into a life that expands our vision quests. We will discover a desire that overwhelms and sanctifies our own wishes. To visualize the possibilists, we realize our obedience to God in love and grace and in the power of lasting joy. John 5:24.

Joy lasts!

Go where God opens doors, even when they closed.

Any person who does not believe the Word of God is now in a state of death even if that one is alive biologically. Remember Jesus' response to Martha. John 11:25-26.

If we truly believe that joy lasts forever, we know God has prepared an eternal home for us. It is a house with many rooms. John 14:1-2. We will live in eternal hope every day. Eternal confidence causes us to live in boldness and freedom.

Our future is secure. God will lead people into an eternal relationship with Christ.

Be encouraged that God is working on our behalf to use our every word and active witness to bring people to the Kingdom. Remember that gospel song, "I Can Imagine." Imagine people revealing that their salvation came as a result of somebody's saving witness. Jude 20-21.

Keats would agree that beauty is like a beautiful shade tree under which we enjoy good health. Every day it is beauty which fills us with the spirit to live joyfully. The Bible assures us that "eternal life" happens because we are joined with our Creator at the root of our existence in the love and grace of God. The gospel and the example of Jesus in the Good News shows us now how to begin what is known as eternal life.

Take a walk and enjoy every step. God reveals love, grace, joy, patience and endurance, gentleness, kindness, faithfulness, goodness, self-control, which are gifts from the Holy Spirit. Our gratitude leads to love.

## Walking the Planet

Nobody knows how long we will have to walk on planet earth, which we call home. As long as we are here, we can walk in beauty and joy.

Without beauty that lasts forever, the world would be filled with cruel and demeaning joyless human beings. Poets such as Keats write about the joy coming from beautiful things on earth. Saint Francis spoke of the sun, moon, trees, birds, and flowers.

Note the sounds in your own life. Feelings of joy may be nature-created: a cardinal's song, water lapping, wind blowing through pine trees, and hearing rain on the roof. I am so grateful for my hearing aids that enable me to hear God's songs in the night, and the words that are opened to me to the delight of all whom I encounter along life's journey.

My books would be so much less without John Killinger's forwards. I have become closer to John than I was with my own father, my brothers, and any of my pastoring colleagues.

I want to end my writing by quoting the last words from one of my favorite books written by John Killinger.

"If you will learn to live this way every day, you will always have a song in your heart and the path before you will be lined with flowers. Joy will spring up inside you like a fountain, and you will lie down to sleep at night with peace in your soul. And you will say,' Blessed be the name of our God forever and everwho calls us to a new rule where righteousness will be the order of the day forever!"' (John Killinger, *Letting God Bless You*, p. 139.

# Bibliography

Algoe, S.B. and Albert Stanton. "Gratitude When It Is Needed Most: Social Function of Gratitude in Women with Metastatic Breast Cancer," *Emotion*, 12:163-168, 2012.

Baumeister, R.F. and M.R. Leary. "The Need to Belong: Desire for Interpersonal Attachments as a Fundamental Human Motivation," *Psychological Bulletin* 117, no. 3, pp. 497-529, 1995.

Buber, Martin. *Tale of the Hasidim: The Early Masters.* New York: Schlocken Books, 1972.

Burton, C.M., and L.A. King, "The Health Benefits of Writing About Intensely Positive Experiences," *Journal of Research in Personality*, 38, 150-173, 2004.

Buxbaum, Y.T. *Jewish Tales of Mystic Joy.* New York: Jossey-Bass Books, 2012.

Chauhan, P.H. and David Leeming, "A Homologic Phenomenological Exploration of Feeling Joyful," *The Journal of Positive Psychology*, Volume 15, number one, pp. 99-106, 2020.

Cottrell, Larry. "Joy and Happiness: A Simultaneous and Evolutionary Concept," *Journal of Advanced Nursing*, 72/7, pp. 1,506-1,517, 2022.

Coakley, Sarah. *A New Association: Sexuality, Gender, and the Quest for God.* New York: Bloomsbury Press, 2019.

Davis, Stephen. *Risen Indeed: Making Sense of the Resurrection.* Grand Rapids, Michigan: Eerdmans, 1993.

Ellul, Jacques. *Hope in a Time of Abandonment*. New York: Seabury Press, 1973.

Fischer, John Martin. "Why Immortality Is Not So Bad," *International Journal of Philosophical Studies*, 2, number 2, 262-267, 2020.

Frazee, Randy and Robert Noland. *Think, Act, Believe Like Jesus: Becoming a New Person in Christ*. Grand Rapids, Michigan: Zondervan, 2014.

Frederickson, Barbara L. "The Role of Positive Emotions in Positive Psychology." *American Psychological Journal*. 56, 218-226, 2002.

Frija, N.H. *The Emotions*. Cambridge: Cambridge University Press, 1986. Fuller, Kristen. "The Difference Between Hearing and Listening," *Psychology Today*, July 8, 2021.

Gendler, Janet Ruth, *The Book of Qualities*. Berkley, California: Turquoise Mountain Publications, 1984.

George, James M. "A Leader's Positive Mood and Organizational Group Work Performance," *Journal of Applied Social Psychology*, 25, 778-798, 1995.

Graham, Samuel, John Durtschi, and M.S. Clark, "The Benefits of Expressing Gratitude to a Partner Changes One's View of the Relationship," *Psychological Science*, 21: pp. 574-580, 2010.

Greeley, Andrew. *Love and Play*. Chicago: Thomas More Publishers, 1975.

Hird, Anne. *Learning from Cyber-Savvy Students: How Internet Age Kids Impact Classroom Teaching*. Sterling, Virginia: Stylus Publishing Company, 2014.

Hoard, G. Richard. *Alone Among the Living*. Athens, Georgia: University of Georgia Press, 1998.

Hough, Samuel. *Kierkegaard's Dancing Tax Collector: Faith, Finitude, and Silence*. Oxford: Oxford University Press, 2019.

Jagodzinski, Cecile M. *Privacy and Printing: Reading and Writing in Seventeenth Century England*. Charlottesville: University Press of the University of Virginia, 2002.

Jeanrold, Werner G. *A Theology of Love*. London: T and T. Clark, 2010.

Jenson, David H. *God, Desire, and a Theology of Human Sexuality*. Louisville, Kentucky: Westminster John Knox Press, 2014.

Johnson, Sue. *Love Sense: The Revolutionary New Science of Romantic Relationships*. New York: Little, Brown and Company Publishers, 2013.

Jonsson, Melissa Joy. *The Art of Limitless Living: The Joy, Possibilities, and Power of Living a Heart-Centered Life*. New York: Weiser Books, 2020.

Keen, Sam. *To a Dancing God*. New York: Harper & Row. 1970.

Kennedy, Billy. *The Scots-Irish in the Shenandoah Valley*. Belfast, Northern Ireland: Ambassador Productions, 1996.

Killinger, John. *Leave It to the Spirit*. San Francisco: Harper & Row, 1971. Killinger, John. *Letting God Bless You: The Beatitudes for Today*. Nashville: Abingdon Press, 1992.

Kunkel, Fritz. *Creation Continues*. Waco, Texas: Word Books, 1973.

Lesiv, Taras. "Francis of Assisi's Perfect Jouissance: Theorizing Conversion through Objects and Affects in Early Franciscan Fragments," *Material Religion: The Journal of Objects, Art, and Belief.* Volume 18, Issue 2, 2022.

Lewis, C.S. *A Grief Observed.* New York: Bantom, 1976.
Lewis, C.S. "Answers to Questions about Christianity," *God in the Dock: Essays on Theology and Ethics.* Grand Rapids, Michigan: Eerdmans Academic Books, 1970.

Lewis, C.S. *Surprised by Joy: The Shape of My Life.* Orlando, Florida: Harcourt, Brace, and World, 1955.

Mace, Nancy L. and Peter V. Rabins. *The 36-Hour Day: A Family Guide to Caring for Persons with Alzheimer Disease, Related Dementing Illnesses, and Memory Loss in Later Life.* Baltimore and London: The Johns Hopkins University Press, 1999.

Malz, Betty. *My Glimpse of Eternity.* Carmel, New York: Guideposts, 1977.

Manskar, Gina. "Cultivating Joy," *Alive Now!* July-August. Nashville: The Upper Room, 2015.

Marney, Carlyle. *The Coming Faith.* Nashville: Abingdon Press, 1970.

Meadows, Chris M. Notes from doctoral level course on joy at Vanderbilt Divinity School in 1972. "Joy: A Review of the Literature and Suggestions for Future Directions," *The Journal of Positive Psychology,* Volume 15, number one, pp. 5-24, 2020.

McGurk, Douglas. "An Examination of the Sermons of Pastor Jean Medard in the French City and District of Rousen, 1939-1945," unpublished dissertation for the doctor of philosophy degree at Queens' University Institute of Theology, Belfast, Northern Ireland, 2022.

McLuhan, Marshall. *Counterblast for Understanding Media: The Extensions of Man.* New York: Harcourt, Brace, and the World Books, 1972.

McRaney, William. *The Art of Personal Evangelism.* Nashville: Broadman and Holman Publishers, 2006.

McReynolds. James. *Black Preaching: Burden of a People.* Nashville: National Baptist Press, 1971.

McReynolds, James. *Dancing with God A Theology of Joy.* Cleveland, Tennessee: Parson's Porch Books, 2016.

McReynolds, James. *Great Is Thy Faithfulness: When Our Faith Is Shaken.* Cleveland, Tennessee: Parson's Porch Books, 2021.

McReynolds, James. *Grace Revealed: Bringing Joy to the World.* Cleveland, Tennessee: Parson's Porch Books, 2022.

McReynolds, James. *Igniting Joy: The Magic of Ordinary People.* Cleveland Tennessee: Parson's Porch Books, 2023.

McReynolds, James. *Joy Beyond the Walls of This World: Healing the Souls of Men … and Women.* Cleveland, Tennessee: Parson's Porch Books, 2021.

McReynolds, James. *Joy Comes in the Mourning: Love Is Forever.* Cleveland, Tennessee: Parson's Porch Books, 2020.
McReynolds, James. *Joy Filled Souls: It Is Well with My Soul.* Cleveland, Tennessee: Parson's Porch Books, 2022.

McReynolds, James. *Joy in All Seasons: Walking Each Other Home to God.* Cleveland Tennessee: Parson's Porch Books, 2021.

McReynolds, James. *Living the Dream: Adventure in Marriage.* Cleveland, Tennessee: Parson's Porch Books, 2021.

McReynolds, *Passionate Joy.* Shanghai, China: Universe Books, Inc. 1999.

McReynolds, James. *Peace that Passes All Understanding.* Cleveland, Tennessee: Parson's Porch Books, 2022.

McReynolds, James. *Quest for Joy: Life Beyond Pleasure and Profit.* Houston, Texas: The Kingwood Publishing Group, 1977.

McReynolds, James. *Spirit of Joy Church.* Cleveland, Tennessee: Parson's Porch Books, 2019.

McReynolds, James. *The Gospel of Joy: Global Impact of the Ministry of Joy to the World.* Cleveland, Tennessee: Parson's Porch Books, 2022.

McReynolds, James. *The Joy of Prayer: The Way of Intimacy with God.* Cleveland, Tennessee: Parson's Porch Books, 2020.

McReynolds, James. *The Joy of Preaching: Encountering Jesus through the Word of God.* Cleveland, Tennessee: Parson's Porch Books, 2013.

McReynolds, *The Joy of the Kingdom: Envisioning the Great Commission.* Cleveland, Tennessee, 2020.

McReynolds, James. *The Power of Joy: Jouissance, Joie de Vivre.* Cleveland, Tennessee: Parson's Porch Books, 2023.

McReynolds, James. *The Power of Kindness: Empathy in a Traumatic World.* Cleveland, Tennessee: Parson's Porch Books, 2023.

McReynolds, James. *The Silence of the Church: The Spiritual Struggle with Sexuality.* Cleveland, Tennessee: Parson's Porch Books, 2017.

McReynolds, James. *The Spirituality of Joy: The* Least *Discussed Human Emotion.* Cleveland, Tennessee: Parson's Porch Books, 2011.

McReynolds, James. *The Strength of Being Tender: Love Is Like a Butterfly.* Cleveland, Tennessee: Parson's Porch Books, 2022.

McReynolds, James. *Visionquest of Joy: The Least Discussed Human Emotion.* Bryn Mawr, Pennsylvania: Dorrance and Company, Incorporated, 1988.

McReynolds, James. *Walking with God in the Garden: Journey to Jouissance.* Cleveland, Tennessee: Parson's Porch Books, 2021.

Meadows, Chris. *A Psychological Perspective on Joy and Emotional Fulfillment.* New York: Rutledge Books, 2014.

Peck, Scott. *Golf and the Spirit of God: Lessons for the Journey.* New York: Three Rivers Press, 2000.

Peterson, Eugene. *A Long Obedience in the Same Direction.* Downers Grove, Illinois: InterVarsity Press, 1999.

Post, Stephen G. *Altruism and Altruistic Love.* New York: Oxford University Press, 2002.

Rawls, John. *A Theory of Justice.* Cambridge, Massachusetts: Harvard University Press, 1971.

Reynolds, William, ed. *Words, Music, and the Church.* Nashville: Abingdon Press, 1968.

Roberts, B.W., Caspi, Albert, and T.E. Moffitt, "Work Experiences and Personality Development in Young Adulthood," *Journal of Personality and Social Psychology*, 84, 582-599, 2003.

Roman, Sandy. *Living with Joy: Keys to Personal Power and Spiritual Transformation*. New York: H.J. Kramer Books, 2022.

Saint John of the Cross, "The Dark Night," *The Collected Works of Saint John of the Cross*. Trans. K. Kavanaugh and O. Rodriguez. Washington, D.C.: ICs Publications, 1991.

Sears, Robert T. "A Theology for Joy and Healing," *The Journal of Christian Healing*, volume 19, Summer issue, pp. 3-22, 1997.

Seligman, M.E.P. *Flourish*. New York: The Free Press, 2012.

Sheehy, Gail. *New Passages*. New York: Random House, 1995.

Sweet, Leonard. *Carpe Manana: Is Your Church Ready to Seize Tomorrow?* Grand Rapids, Michigan: Zondervan Books, 2001.

Sweet, Leonard. *The Dawn Mistaken for Dusk: If God So Loved the World, Why Can't We?* Grand Rapids, Michigan: Zondervan Books, 1999.

Walls, Jerry. "Heaven: The Logic of Eternal Joy," *Ars Disputandi*, Volume 4, Oxford: Oxford University Press, 2002.

Watkins, Philip, Robert Emmons, and Joshua Bell, "Joy Is a Distinct Emotion: Assessment of Joy and Relationship to Gratitude and Well- Being," *Positive Psychology*, volume 10, pp. 1-90, December 2017.

Wood, A.M. "Gratitude and Well-Being: A Review and Theoretical Orientation," *Clinical Psychology Review*, volume 30, pp. 890-905, 2002.

# About the Author

James McReynolds' passionate love for Jesus powerfully imports the joy of the Lord wherever he goes. His calling is to bring glory to God by loving others like Jesus loves him.

Jim celebrated 70 years of ministry in 2023. Millions have heard him preach, read his books, listened his radio and television presentations. As a licensed psychotherapist with a doctor of psychology degree, he deeply believes that souls are made for endurance. Jim is an associate member of the American Association of Marriage and Family Therapists. He is a charter member of the American Association of Christian Counselors

Jim's long ministry has revolutionized the lives of countless people. Dr. Norman Vincent Peale, preacher of positive thinking at Marble Collegiate Church in New York anointed him as the Minister of Joy to the World.

McReynolds believes his world travels to share joy have been miracles from God. Agnes Hull, one of Jim's English professor at Carson-Newman University got him in touch with Charles Trentham, pastor, First Baptist Church in Knoxville, Tennessee. He served that church as student minister of prayer.

McReynolds is now a retired elder in full membership in the Holston Conference of the United Methodist Church. He is also retired from the Baptist and Christian Church (Disciples of Christ) denominations.

Jim used his talents and gifts in service to Christ at the Sunday School Board of the Southern Baptist Convention. He was elected the moderator of the Nebraska Region of the Christian Church. Jim has now earned five doctorates and a total of nine degrees.

He served as a graduate assistant in psychology of religion at Baylor University in Waco, Texas. He earned a bachelor of journalism from the University of Missouri in Columbia. His master of religious education degree is from Midwestern Baptist Theological Seminary in Kansas City, Missouri. His master and doctor of divinity degrees were earned at the Vanderbilt University Divinity School in Nashville, Tennessee. His doctor of psychology is from the Graduate Theological Foundation including studies and research at Christ College of the University of Oxford and internship at the Appalachian Counseling Center on the King University campus in Bristol, Tennessee.

In 2023, Jim celebrated his 70th anniversary as a preacher with receptions in Elmwood for his Platinum Jubilee. He has 108,065 sermons stored in his basement. He once went 18,396 days, 50 years, four months, and 12 days preaching at least one sermon. He has been a prolific author.

He does none of his ministry to impress, but for the world to delight in Jesus the Christ, and to honor him and give Jesus the glory. The gospel of John ends by saying that Jesus was and is limitless. All the world could not contain the books that could be written.

Contact the author at:

320 North Fourth Street, Elmwood, Nebraska 68349.

He receives email at joyminister@windstream.net.

Phone number: 1-402- 994-2370.